Field-Based Learning in Family Life Education

Tara Newman • Ashley Schmitt
Editors

Field-Based Learning in Family Life Education

Facilitating High-Impact Experiences in Undergraduate Family Science Programs

Editors
Tara Newman
University of Southern Queensland
Toowoomba, Queensland, Australia

Ashley Schmitt
Texas A&M University
College Station, Texas, USA

ISBN 978-3-319-81985-3   ISBN 978-3-319-39874-7 (eBook)
DOI 10.1007/978-3-319-39874-7

© The Editor(s) (if applicable) and The Author(s) 2017
Softcover reprint of the hardcover 1st edition 2016
This work is subject to copyright. All rights are solely and exclusively licensed by the Publisher, whether the whole or part of the material is concerned, specifically the rights of translation, reprinting, reuse of illustrations, recitation, broadcasting, reproduction on microfilms or in any other physical way, and transmission or information storage and retrieval, electronic adaptation, computer software, or by similar or dissimilar methodology now known or hereafter developed.
The use of general descriptive names, registered names, trademarks, service marks, etc. in this publication does not imply, even in the absence of a specific statement, that such names are exempt from the relevant protective laws and regulations and therefore free for general use.
The publisher, the authors and the editors are safe to assume that the advice and information in this book are believed to be true and accurate at the date of publication. Neither the publisher nor the authors or the editors give a warranty, express or implied, with respect to the material contained herein or for any errors or omissions that may have been made.

Cover image © Blend Images / Alamy Stock Photo

Printed on acid-free paper

This Palgrave Macmillan imprint is published by Springer Nature
The registered company is Springer International Publishing AG
The registered company address is: Gewerbestrasse 11, 6330 Cham, Switzerland

Foreword

The text *Field-Based Learning in Family Life Education: Facilitating High-Impact Experiences in Undergraduates Family Science Programs* is a brilliant, invigorating, and refreshing piece of scholarship. Not only is it worthy of attention but also timely and needed to further enhance the quality of undergraduate and graduate family science programs.

Anyone who reads this work will gain a broad, rejuvenating perspective on the significance of internship and practicum experiences, as well as the integration of service learning and community-based experiences. Internship and practicum experiences provide students at the undergraduate and graduate level an opportunity to have "hands-on experiences," while service learning and community-based experiences are more of an application phase through service learning with community-based organizations.

This text is composed of two sections that are skillfully written by numerous contributors. Each contributor painstakingly writes on divergent topics, yet there is a thread of commonalty throughout the entire topics inherent within each section. The first section focuses specifically on internship and practicum experiences. The chapters in this section begin with the role of practicum in undergraduate education, professional sequence and high impact, personal and professional development, effectively placing family studies majors at internship sites, and learning to observe and interpret behavior within family courses. This section is excellent as it purports the value of internship and practicum experiences.

The second section consists of chapters with heavy emphasis on service learning and community-based experiences. The chapters in this section focus on community-based learning in a particular context, followed by additional chapters on students in human service programs, service learning design, service learning high-impact strategies in undergraduate family science programming, service learning in a helping skills course, and teaching grant writing to undergraduate students. The implication of this section bridges the gap between theory and practice.

Dr. Newman and the contributors are to be commended for this seminal work that is a "breath of fresh air" to family science programs. It is one of the best sources I have viewed in my two decades as a marriage and family sociologist!

David L. Briscoe, Ph.D., CFLE, FAGHE, DFSSA, FFAGS, FSVHE

Professor of Sociology, Graduate School Faculty, and Distinguished Teaching Fellow

College of Arts, Humanities, and Social Sciences

Department of Sociology and Anthropology

University of Arkansas at Little Rock

Contents

1. Exploring High-Impact Educational Experiences in Higher Education — 1
   Tara Newman

Part I Internship and Practicum Experiences — 7

2. The Role of Practicum in Undergraduate Family Life Education — 9
   Linda S. Behrendt

3. The Professional Sequence and High-Impact Teaching: The Introductory Course — 19
   Deborah C. Bailey, Kimberly Tate

4. The Professional Sequence and High-Impact Teaching: Skills, Methods, and Internships — 29
   Edgar C. J. Long, Deborah C. Bailey

5. Personal and Professional Development Through Internship Engagement — 39
   Maria K. Schmidt

6 Effectively Placing Family Studies Majors
   at Internship Sites: The ECU-LINCS Match Process   51
   *Alan C. Taylor, Elizabeth B. Carroll, Sharon M. Ballard,
   Eboni J. Baugh, Bryce L. Jorgensen*

7 Developing Connections: Using an On-Campus
   Event to Connect HDFS Students and the Community   61
   Laura Landry-Meyer, Michael R. Sturm Jr.

8 Learning to Observe and Interpret Behavior as a
   High-Impact Practice Within Family Science Courses   73
   Dave Riley

9 Learning Through Engagement: A Praxis Approach
   to Teaching Family Life Education Methodology   81
   Nathan R. Cottle, Jeremy Boden, Grant Richards

Part II Service Learning and Community-Based Experiences   89

10 Community-Based Learning with Young Children
    in a Child Development Center   91
    Mary A. Sciaraffa

11 Family Life Education with Diverse Community Partners   111
    Jonathan Davis, Celeste Hill, Kristie Chandler

12 Interprofessional Field-Based Learning in a Program
    Planning and Evaluation Course for Students
    in Human Service Programs   121
    Charlene VanLeeuwen

13 Perspective Transformation via Service-Learning
    in Family Life Education Methodology   133
    Scott Tobias

14	Reverse Planning a Service Learning Activity for an Undergraduate Public Policy Course *Jacki Fitzpatrick*	143
15	Service-Learning Design Through a Management Model *Kendra Brandes, G. Kevin Randall, Lauren Leach-Steffens*	153
16	Service Learning in Family Life Education: Incorporating High-Impact Strategies in Undergraduate Family Science Programming *Anita Glee Bertram, Brandon Burr*	165
17	Service Learning in a Helping Skills Course *Jennifer Dobbs-Oates*	175
18	Teaching Grant Writing to Undergraduate Students: A High-Impact Experience *Bryce L. Jorgensen, Sharon M. Ballard, Eboni Baugh, Alan Taylor, Elizabeth Carroll*	185
19	Conclusion *Ashley Schmitt*	193

Appendix A: Writing Assignment Questions from the Role of Practicum in Undergraduate Family Life Education — 199

Appendix B: Rubrics, Assignments, Evaluations, and Reflections from Community-Based Learning with Young Children in a Child Development Center — 201

Index — 215

List of Contributors

Deborah C. Bailey, CFLE, LMFT is an Associate Professor of Human Development and Family Studies at Central Michigan University in Mt Pleasant, MI.

Sharon M. Ballard, CFLE is an Associate Professor and Chair in the Department of Child Development and Family Relations at East Carolina University in Greenville, NC.

Eboni J. Baugh, CFLE is an Assistant Professor and Program Coordinator of Family and Community Services in the Department of Human Development and Family Science at East Carolina University in Greenville, NC.

Linda S. Behrendt is an Associate Professor in the Department of Applied Health Sciences at Indiana State University in Terre Haute, IN.

Anita Glee Bertram, CFLE, CCCS is an Associate Professor in Human Environmental Sciences at the University of Central Oklahoma in Edmond, OK.

Jeremy Boden is a Lecturer in Family Studies at Utah Valley University in Orem, UT.

Kendra Brandes is an Associate Professor in the Department of Family and Consumer Sciences at Bradley University in Peoria, IL.

Brandon Burr, CFLE is an Assistant Professor in Human Environmental Sciences at the University of Central Oklahoma in Edmond, OK.

Elizabeth B. Carroll, J.D., CFLE is an Associate Professor of Child Development and Family Relations at East Carolina University, Greenville, NC.

Kristie Chandler is Chair and Associate Professor in the Department of Human Development and Family Life Education at Samford University in Birmingham, AL.

Nathan R. Cottle is a Professor of Family Studies at Utah Valley University in Orem, UT.

Jonathan Davis is an Associate Professor in the Department of Human Development and Family Life Education at Samford University in Birmingham, AL.

Jennifer Dobbs-Oates is a Clinical Assistant Professor in the Department of Human Development and Family Studies at Purdue University in West Lafayette, IN.

Jacki Fitzpatrick is an Associate Professor of Family Studies at Texas Tech University in Lubbock, TX.

Celeste Hill is an Assistant Academic Advisor and Instructor in the Department of Human Development and Family Life Education at Samford University in Birmingham, AL.

Bryce L. Jorgensen, CFLE is an Assistant Professor and Family Resource Management Specialist in the Department of Extension Family and Consumer Sciences at New Mexico State University in Las Cruces, NM.

Laura Landry-Meyer, CFLE is an Associate Professor of Human Development and Family Studies at Bowling Green State University in Bowling Green, OH.

Lauren Leach-Steffens is an Associate Professor in the Department of Behavioral Sciences at Northwest Missouri State University in Maryville, MO.

Edgar C. J. Long, LMFT is a Professor of Human Development and Family Studies at Central Michigan University in Mt Pleasant, MI.

G. Kevin Randall, CFLE is a Scientist at the Partnerships in Prevention Science Institute in Ames, IW.

Grant Richards is a Professor of Family Studies at Utah Valley University in Orem, UT.

Dave Riley is the Rothermel-Bascom Professor of Human Ecology at the University of Wisconsin-Madison in Madison, WI.

Maria K. Schmidt, CFLE is an Assistant Professor and Internship Coordinator in the School of Public Health-Bloomington working with Human Development and Family Studies and Youth Development at Indiana University in Bloomington, IN.

Mary A. Sciaraffa, CFLE is an Associate Professor in Child and Family Studies at Eastern Kentucky University in Richmond, KY.

Michael R. Sturm Jr., MFT, CFLE is an Instructor in Human Development and Family Studies at Bowling Green State University in Bowling Green, OH.

Kimberly Tate is a Graduate Student in Human Development and Family Studies at Central Michigan University in Mt Pleasant, MI.

Alan C. Taylor, CFLE is an Assistant Professor in the Department of Child Development and Family Relations at East Carolina University in Greenville, NC.

Scott Tobias is an Assistant Professor of Human Development and Family Studies at Kent State University at Stark in North Canton, OH.

Charlene VanLeeuwen, M.Ed., CFLE, ABD is an Instructor and Field Placement Coordinator in the Department of Applied Human Sciences at the University of Prince Edward Island, Charlottetown, Prince Edward Island, Canada.

List of Figures

Fig. 11.1	Course Objectives	114
Fig. 15.1	Taxonomy of significant learning. Adapted from *Creating significant learning experiences: An integrated approach to designing college courses*, by L.D. Fink, 2003, p. 30. Copyright 2003 by Jossey-Bass, San Francisco, CA	155
Fig. 15.2	The resource management model. Adapted from *Resource management for individuals and families*, by E.B. Goldsmith, 2010, p. 6. Copyright 2010 by Prentice Hall	156

List of Tables

Table 12.1	Course Objectives	124
Table 13.1	Mezirow's Phases of Transformation	134
Table 15.1	Six Attributes of Effective High-Impact Programs	154
Table 15.2	Service-Learning Design Through a Management Model	159

CHAPTER 1

Exploring High-Impact Educational Experiences in Higher Education

Tara Newman

When George Kuh first began talking about high-impact educational experiences, he was quick to point out that while such practices were available across many campuses and programs, they were largely unsystematic (Kuh, 2008). This lack of systemic focus indicates that higher education as a whole may not be adapting as quickly as individual educators are. Instructors seem to understand (whether through empirical studies or just their "gut feeling") that for their students to fully benefit from their educational journey, there must be some degree of learner activity involved, and they have incorporated some degree of active learning accordingly. This enthusiasm for active learning spans across disciplines and across cultures (e.g. Li & Wu, 2015; Niemi & Nevgi, 2014; Pineda-Báez et al., 2014). Indeed, the literature is replete with studies demonstrating that "the time and energy students devote to educationally purposeful activities is the single best predictor of learning and personal development" during the university experience (Kuh, Kinzie, Schuh, & Whitt, 2005, p. 8).

In a recent study of US employers, participants strongly endorsed active learning practices and overwhelmingly expressed preference for educational experiences that require learners to apply and develop skills

T. Newman (✉)
University of Southern Queensland, Toowoomba, QLD, Australia

over those activities that focus on individual pockets of knowledge (Hart Research Associates, 2013). Not only are such practices increasingly preferred by employers, but institutions discovered decades ago that engaging students in such ways results in a deeper sense of commitment to the institution, improved retention, better grades, and higher graduation rates (Astin, 1993). With the current commercialized context of higher education, especially in the United States, these outcomes are progressively important to the enrollment figures and graduation rates upon which much funding and accountability measures are linked.

In the report, *College Learning for a New Global Century* (AAC&U, 2007), the Association of American Colleges and Universities (AAC&U) listed ten of the more promising "high-impact" practices. The practices identified include a mix of activities including first-year seminars, learning communities, service learning, undergraduate research, study abroad, internships, and capstone courses/projects. While they are listed separately, high-impact educational practices are united by the six significant components. When engaged in high-impact practices (HIP) activities, students:

- devote considerable amounts of time and effort to purposeful tasks;
- interact with faculty and peers about substantive matters;
- experience diversity through contact with people who are different than themselves;
- get frequent feedback about their performance;
- see how what they are learning works in different settings, on and off the campus; and
- connect personally and professionally through opportunities for active, collaborative learning (AAC&U, 2007).

In Family Sciences programs, one can find examples of a variety of educational experiences that incorporate many or all of these elements, as the discipline tends to be very people-centric and applied in nature. However, this book is exploring programs with systems designed to ensure, that by placing students directly in the field, they will encounter authentic, high-impact opportunities to positively influence families across the lifespan at the very beginning of their career. The implementation models advocated have many different names (work-integrated learning, internships, service learning, or practicum, to name a few), with key commonalities:

- Each learning experience strives to incorporate the elements of high-impact educational practices; and
- Each of them occurs embedded within an authentic context in the field, with all of the complexities that come from interactions with real-life human beings.

The overarching term used in this book—field-based learning—is designed to incorporate most models that extend the walls of the classroom to engage students directly in the field of their chosen career path. In this volume, the field-based learning activities are those that are specific to Family Studies and/or Family Life Education.

The discipline of Family Life Education is one that is extremely diverse, and graduates must enter the workforce prepared with transferrable skills in a given set of content areas (Cassidy, 2009; Darling & Cassidy, 2014; Darling, Fleming, & Cassidy, 2009). While not all Family Life Educators (FLE) accept a position with the same job title, for well over a decade, businesses have been acknowledging the work of FLE as valuable to their employees' productivity through the implementation of family life programming within the organization (Galinsky, Bond, & Hill, 2004). In order for new professionals to develop the skills to immediately contribute in their roles as Family Life Educators, it is essential they have the opportunity to learn in authentic and supported contexts, as there is a great possibility that there will not be another FLE in the work environment or even locally to provide mentoring or support.

The contextually authentic learning experiences are so important to the preparation of Family Life Educators that the National Council on Family Relations (NCFR), who sponsors the Certified Family Life Educator (CFLE) credential, requires their approved programs to have an experiential learning opportunity in the field with a minimum of 120 direct contact hours in Family Life Education practice. Those who are seeking full certification as a CFLE postgraduation from a non-approved program must be able to demonstrate a minimum of 3200 hours of work experience (NCFR, 2015). These field-based learning experiences are essential to the Family Life Educator's understanding of the complexities in the discipline and enable them to synthesize the skills and content learned throughout their educational program.

While there is a growing body of theoretical literature on high-impact practices (HIP) and their benefit to student outcomes, there is little that actually guides faculty on the development of HIP classroom experiences.

Simultaneously, there is a demand for discipline-specific exploration into how the elements of high-impact practice manifest themselves on the university campus. In my work promoting high-impact pedagogy, faculty often express confusion about how their practice aligned with that advocated by Kuh (2008). I am asked similar questions wherever I go to speak on high-impact pedagogy:

- How is "frequent feedback" defined and how does one provide meaningful feedback more frequently in large classes?
- What does it "look like" when faculty and peers interact about substantive matters? Who decides what is substantive?
- How does one ensure that the assigned tasks are purposeful in the eyes of the learner and how can one be sure students are devoting considerable amounts of time and effort to them?
- How do I actually DO these kinds of activities with students? It seems so complex!

The list goes on and on. Faculty want to implement high-impact practices, but are not always able to identify how to do so effectively. In the discipline of Family Science, in particular, where faculty are largely preparing future Family Life Educators, a high value is placed on applying the ten NCFR-identified key content areas to promote healthy families through a preventative approach (National Council on Family Relations, 2014). The idea for this book results from the many questions I received as a member of two national-level NCFR committees (CFLE Advisory Board and the Annual Program Review Committee) and my work as an institutional consultant in the development of high-impact initiatives. It is my intent that the book will serve as a resource for faculty and program leaders who are interested in incorporating high-impact practices into their Family Science and Family Life Education programming.

To this end, the text provides case studies as examples for those seeking to systematize high-impact educational experiences with emerging practitioners in family-related disciplines. Presented by leading scholars in the field of family life education, this book provides successful models for field-based learning experiences in Family Life Education. Each chapter provides an overview of the implementation details, including key points that others developing a plan could use to guide their thinking. In addition, each chapter is grounded in previous scholarship and identifies how the elements of high-impact practices are addressed within a specific institutional context. Contributors share their experiences implementing service learning, internships/practice, and other educational platforms outside the classroom walls.

Readers will find that the book addresses both specific content areas within family life education (such as Human Growth and Development across the Lifespan or Family Life Education Methodology) and general course management strategies (such as managing frequent feedback or high-enrollment classes). Its aims are multifaceted. First, I hope that readers will enhance their understanding of the elements of high-impact practices in Family Studies and, specifically, Family Life Education. "Effective" teaching can be a somewhat abstract concept. As chapter authors share their experiences with others, I am hopeful that readers will be able to generate ideas that are appropriate in their own context, thereby enhancing the preparation of future Family Life Educators.

Second, the literature indicates that students who have these experiences have the kinds of outcomes that most educators and institutions desire for their students (higher GPAs, retention rates, and graduation rates, as well as improved learning). In the ever-increasing era of accountability in higher education, it is hoped that readers will be able to apply some of what they read to address targeted institutional and program outcomes. Third, it is my hope that educators will find an increase in their enthusiasm for teaching as a result of the inspiration they receive when reading the projects of their colleagues.

High-impact programming requires intentionality and collaboration, both within and across disciplines, and must be implemented with a focused effort on the part of institutions, rather than by happenstance. As Kuh et al. (2005) state,

> Too often…[high-quality learning environments] are products of serendipity or efforts on the part of students themselves…Moreover, for every student who has such an experience, there are others who do not connect in meaningful ways with their teachers, their peers, or take advantage of learning opportunities. As a result, many students leave school prematurely, or put so little effort into their learning that they fall short of benefiting from college to the extent they should. (p. 9 and 10)

As educators responsible for preparing future generations of FLE professionals and ensuring the viability of FLE as a profession, it is imperative that Family Science programs develop and offer the types of purposeful, field-based learning activities described so openly by the authors in this text. I wish you many moments of inspiration and motivation as you learn more about our colleagues' experiences with their undergraduate students.

References

American Association of Colleges and Universities (AAC&U). (2007). *College learning for the new global century: A report from the national leadership council for liberal education and America's promise.* Washington, DC: Association of American Colleges and Universities.

Astin, A. (1993). *What matters in college: Four critical years revisited.* San Francisco, CA: Jossey-Bass.

Cassidy, D. (2009). Challenges in FLE: Defining and promoting the profession. In D. J. Bredehoft & M. J. Walcheski (Eds.), *Family life education: Integrating theory and practice.* Minneapolis, MN: National Council on Family Relations.

Darling, C., & Cassidy, D. (2014). *Family life education: Working with families across the lifespan* (3rd ed.). Long Grove, IL: Waveland Press.

Darling, C., Fleming, W. M., & Cassidy, D. (2009). Professionalization of family life education: Defining the field. *Family Relations, 58,* 330–345.

Galinsky, E., Bond, J. T., & Hill, E. J. (2004). When work works: A status report on workplace flexibility: Who has it? Who wants it? What difference does it make? Retrieved from http://familiesandwork.org/3w/research/downloads/status.pdf

Hart Research Associates. (2013). *It takes more than a major: Employer priorities for college learning and student success.* Washington, DC: Association of American Colleges and Universities and Hart Research Associates.

Kuh, G. (2008). *High-impact educational practices: What they are, who has access to them, and why they matter.* Washington, DC: AAC&U Publishing.

Kuh, G., Kinzie, J., Schuh, J., & Whitt, E. (2005). *Student success in college: Creating conditions that matter.* San Francisco, CA: Jossey-Bass.

Li, J., & Wu, J. (2015). Active learning for discovery and innovation in criminology with Chinese learners. *Innovations in Education and Teaching International, 52*(2), 113–124. doi:10.1080/14703297.2013.796720.

National Council on Family Relations. (2014). Family life education content areas. Retrieved from https://www.ncfr.org/sites/default/files/downloads/news/fle_content_areas_2014.pdf

National Council on Family Relations. (2015). Work experience for full certification. Retrieved from https://www.ncfr.org/cfle-certification/become-certified/work-experience-full-certification

Niemi, H., & Nevgi, A. (2014). Research studies and active learning promoting professional competences in Finnish teacher education. *Teaching & Teacher Education, 43,* 131–142. doi:10.1016/j.tate.2014.07.006.

Pineda-Báez, C., Bermúdez-Aponte, J., Rubiano-Bello, Á., Pava-García, N., Suárez-García, R., & Cruz-Becerra, F. (2014). Students' engagement and academic performance in the Colombian university context. *Relieve, 20*(2), 1–19. doi:10.7203/relieve.20.2.4238.

PART I

Internship and Practicum Experiences

CHAPTER 2

The Role of Practicum in Undergraduate Family Life Education

Linda S. Behrendt

Undergraduate Human Development and Family Studies (HDFS) majors at Indiana State University are overwhelmingly traditional-age college students with limited experience working with individuals and families across the life span. In addition, HDFS is most often a "found" major; that is, students tend to come to the major from other disciplines and colleges across campus. In initial advising meetings, students talk about their desire to work with people or to work with children; their actual experience is typically limited to working with young children. The HDFS major initially offered an internship experience as an elective. Unstructured and requiring only completion of hours regardless of how they were fulfilled, internship was viewed as an excellent choice by students who wanted upper-level credit without having to take an actual class. Foundational to the development of a quality internship program were an identified focus and stated outcomes for the experience (O'Neill, 2010). Focus and outcomes supported the integration of *high-impact practices* (HIPs) in revising the curriculum, in an effort to improve the quality of education in preparing students for graduation and ultimately career success (Kuh, 2008). Simply put, HIPs are "educational practices that research demonstrates have an

---

L.S. Behrendt (✉)
Department of Applied Health Sciences, Indiana State University, Terre Haute, IN, USA

© The Author(s) 2017
T. Newman, A. Schmitt (eds.), *Field-Based Learning in Family Life Education*, DOI 10.1007/978-3-319-39874-7_2

impact on student learning outcomes and progress toward graduation" (McNair & Albertine, 2012, p. 4). Four of the six HIPs will be addressed in this chapter: *frequent performance feedback, application to other settings, experiencing diversity,* and *authentic connections.* A pre-internship requirement, referred to as practicum, has employed these HIPs to create a stronger major, in turn more effectively equipping graduates for careers in family life education.

2.1   Experiential Learning Across the Curriculum

The need to provide both breadth and depth of experience across the life span guided curriculum revision in 2006. Creation of program outcomes directed expectations across the major, from entry-level courses to senior-level course work. Starting students out in their comfort zone, necessary courses taken early in the major require observation of children from birth to age five. The next level of course work sends students into the community to interact with older children and adolescents who are culturally and/or socio-economically different from them.

The requirement of a practicum experience separate from and prior to internship was designed to continue the breadth of experience begun in the lower-level classes, as well as to begin focusing on professional awareness of attitudes, practices, and expectations. In addition to weekly class meetings, students complete two different experiences of 60 hours each at assigned sites in the local community. Students begin the semester at one site and are rotated to a new assignment at mid-semester. Every student completes one rotation working with elders, a population the majority of students have no experience with and often many pre-conceived ideas. The other rotation depends upon the student's interests and previous experiences. The aim is consistently to broaden students' experiences across the life span and with individuals and families different from themselves. Practicum requirements guide students in their interactions with their on-site supervisor, with self-reflection, professional behaviors, and expectations. Graduation exit interviews have evinced that the experience, learning, and insight gained through the two practicum placements positively influences the choices students make regarding their internship. The overall results of the practicum influence are a stronger commitment to family life education and the applicability of skills and networking opportunities through the internship experience.

For the traditional-age college student, experience across the life span typically comes from jobs such as babysitting, day care, and after school child-care. Experience working with adults and elders is limited, usually to onetime volunteer events. Students are required to take three semesters of developmental course work across the life span. In the course of these semesters, human systems theories, physical, cognitive, social, and emotional development, are covered, and students are required to complete observations and assignments which require them to interact with adolescents and adults on simple projects.

2.2 Life Span Experience Through Practicum

Eighteen- to twenty-two-year-old students have spent the great majority of their lives attending school, an age-segregated experience. Often these educational years are also with individuals whose beliefs, socio-economic status, and race/ethnicity are very similar to their own. Social and work experiences are within the realm of personal comfort; students' choices do not usually move them to be involved in experiences that may evoke uncomfortable or nervous reactions. The purpose of the practicum requirement prior to internship is to build experience based upon the foundational knowledge of development taught in lower-level course work. In addition, the practicum experiences allow the opportunity for interactions outside the choices students may have made in the past. Alex-Assensoh and Ryan (2008) assert that the value of off-campus learning opportunities "inspire student interest in the larger world" (p. 34).

Over the course of the semester, students complete two six-week placements. The placement of students into practicum sites is made based on student input and instructor assessment of each student's experiential and learning needs. Assessment of students' interest, past personal and work experiences, and the needs and makeup of the practicum sites are taken into consideration when placing students. Seeking to diversify each student's experience sometimes leads to what may appear to be odd placements. Providing the opportunity to work with a different age group, socio-economic status, culture, and the like can at the least stretch students boundaries of comfort, and at best open their hearts and minds to work with a population not previously considered.

2.2.1 High-Impact Elements

The *experience of diversity* is considered an element of high-impact practice—creating opportunities for students to come into contact with individuals who are different than themselves. Students' placements at practicum sites where they will interact with people who are different from them are deliberately made. Examples of diversity experienced through practicum include age, socio-economic status, ethnicity, education level, and race.

The opportunity to *create and be involved with authentic connections with peers, faculty, and community* is another high-impact practice employed in practicum. Working together as a cohort in the practicum experience allows students, faculty, site supervisors, staff, and the individuals served through the agency or organization to interact in unique ways. The dynamic between students and faculty differs from typical classroom interactions during weekly meetings where students lead discussions. Together students, faculty, and site supervisors create a learning contract, outlining skills to be gained and the methods to accomplish them. Students assigned to the same site engage in unique tasks together; when students switch to their second site at mid-semester, they share stories and provide updates with the students who were at the site the first six weeks. Close connections are built between student and site supervisor as well as between student and clients.

2.3 Acquisition of Professional Skills

As a group, practicum students meet face-to-face for one hour each week, which assists in creating a sense of cohesion and identity as a group. As noted by Donnelly-Smith (2010), the importance of creating a cohort experience is helpful to overall learning. During this meeting, students' have the opportunity to interact with their peers and the university supervisor on assigned discussion topics which connect family law, public policy, and the needs at their assigned site. In a study of entry-level family life educators, Darling, Fleming, and Cassidy (2009) found that knowledge of family law and public policy was important to effectively meeting needs in families. In addition, the practicum requirement addresses the students' perceived skills needed for obtaining a job (Jaschik, 2010).

There are a limited number of appropriate sites related to family life education within the community; therefore, it is not unusual for a site to host two students at a time for practicum. Two students at a site provides them the opportunity to work together on projects assigned by either their site or university supervisor. A writing assignment requiring students to interview their on-site supervisor for details regarding his/her education, job description, the history of the agency, and funding information provides the opportunity for extended conversation between site supervisor and student.

The addition of the practicum experience as a pre-requisite to internship allows for early development of professional skills not able to be gained in the classroom setting. The structure of the practicum semester is focused on assisting students in understanding professional practice issues and offering the opportunity to practice the skills that will be expected of them as they enter their careers in a short six months. The opportunity to be involved in meaningful work that will translate to resume-building skills is critical to learning experiences (Donnelly-Smith, 2010). Acquisition of basic professional skills provides a foundation upon which the internship experience can build, creating the opportunity for maximum pre-professional preparation. Most students have held jobs, typically hourly positions; most likely their coworkers were others in their age cohort (Steinberg, 2010). Adolescents most often are employed in service (fast-food restaurants) or retail positions where they work with other adolescents and may be supervised by someone only a few years older than themselves (Steinberg, 2010). Moving into careers where students will have coworkers across the age span, young professionals will benefit from communication and interpersonal skill training. While students may believe that they know the expectations in the workforce, their previous interactions with a supervisor who was likely to be within a few years of their age means they may believe that it is appropriate to text or send casual e-mails regarding work-related concerns. Students may not fully realize that resolution of workplace issues requires skills different from those used with friends or even coworkers at previous jobs. The afternoon nap, decisions about whether to go to class, whether to participate in the classroom, scheduling of classes to accommodate late nights are all "perks" of college life; however, these perks are short-lived in the world of work. College students fantasize about life after college—that they will not be as busy, stressed out, or short on time. Practicum requires students to commit to being at their sites at specific scheduled times on a regular basis. Students must complete a set number of hours each week in order to finish 120 hours over the course of the semester. It is not enough to just show up at the practicum site; students must be at their best and ready to perform on task.

2.3.1 High-Impact Elements

The high-impact practice of developing *authentic connections with peers/faculty/community* is employed in the development of professional skills in practicum. A unique relationship is established between instructor and student in the weekly face-to-face meetings, as the students bear responsibility for leading discussions. The creation of a learning contract and completion of tasks assists the student and site supervisor to develop a mentoring relationship. The *application to other settings on and off campus* is the second high-impact practice embodied in the practicum semester. The development of the communication and professional behaviors gained in practicum translate to the internship experience and family life education employment after graduation.

2.4 REFLECTION THROUGH JOURNALING

The role of reflective journaling in experiential learning has been shown to be an effective learning tool (Evans & Mori, 2005), and interactive journaling is a foundational activity for practicum students. Thornton Moore (2010) and Eyler (2009) assert that reflection is necessary in order to create connections between classroom learning and skills gained through experiential learning. Use of an electronic journal feature (e.g., in Blackboard) allows students to record and reflect on their experiences and provides access to the university supervisor for one-on-one conversation and the ability to provide frequent feedback. The option of using an on-line journal allows college students to record their experiences in a familiar format—electronically. Instructor access to each student's on-line journal allows for conversation, fairly immediate feedback, and the ability to assess student growth, an important practice for effective experiential learning (Eyler, 2009). In addition, using on-line journaling provides students the opportunity to practice professional communication skills as they interact with the university supervisor (Mirrer, 2010).

2.4.1 High-Impact Elements

On-line journaling allows for *frequent performance feedback*, a high-impact practice. Using the Blackboard journal option, faculty can read student journals often, and the software allows for written feedback as well as back-and-forth communication. The on-line journals provide the date and time of entry, so as faculty read journal entries, it is evident whether students are recording and reflecting on their experiences in a timely manner.

2.5 Family Service Interviews

Central to the practicum experiences is an investigative interview assignment. This assignment assists students' understanding regarding the realities of family service agencies, requiring them to investigate questions that they might not otherwise consider until they enter the field of family life education as a professional. This exercise assists students in understanding the difference between non- and for-profit agencies, important in career decision-making.

Information regarding the history and mission of the agency are foundational to understanding the day-to-day operations as well as contemplation of future work in that or a similar agency or organization. Funding information reveals methods of support for the agency, such as fee-for-service, grants, or the United Way. Knowledge of funding also informs students how budget decisions are made, and perhaps provides understanding about staffing decisions and employee pay scales.

The target population that the practicum site aims to serve is another item students must investigate in the writing project. The population being served may seem obvious; however, the interplay of the mission and funding of the agency along with the population being served brings deeper insight into how the agency or organization works. Seeking to serve a population above or below the average cost of living in a community could point to choices made for programming, staffing, and the like.

Agencies and organizations rarely exist in a vacuum within the community; they depend on networking with supportive and perhaps even competitive agencies. Sharing resources and information is an important practice in meeting the needs of the agencies' target populations. Firsthand knowledge of the importance of networking points students to facts they will need for future positions. While the names of the resources may be different, the understanding and process is similar across family service agencies. Answering questions regarding community networking also broadens students' knowledge of the agencies and organizations within the human services field.

The last area of focus in the writing assignment concerns the education required for various positions at their practicum site. Interviewing an employee at both the bachelor's and master's levels gives students a realistic perspective regarding career expectations and, depending upon their career aspirations, the need for further education.

2.5.1 High-Impact Elements

The writing assignment employs the high-impact practice of *applying learning to other settings both on and off campus*. Information gathered through the written project may be applied to other agencies, to future course work including traditional classes as well as internship, and to organizations which the student is involved (e.g., Greek life, faith-based groups). Often students learn a great deal about other organizations through the networking question, which is information that is carried over to future family life education agencies.

CONCLUSION

Use of HIPs in the first level of experiential learning for Human Development and Family Life majors has been beneficial to overall student learning as well as influencing student performance in the internship semester. The broader focus of the practicum and the use of HIPs have been beneficial to overall student learning as well as influencing student performance in the internship semester. *Frequent performance feedback*, the opportunity to *create and be involved with authentic connections with peers, faculty, and community, experience diversity*, and *apply learning to other settings both on and off campus* have assisted students in gaining skills and applying knowledge in real-life settings. Life doesn't happen in neatly arranged chapters, logically compartmentalized for exams. The transfer of knowledge from textbooks and classrooms to real life, guided by HIPs, has aided students in being ready to invest themselves fully and realistically in an internship that will point them toward an appropriate career path in family life education.

REFERENCES

Alex-Assensoh, Y., & Ryan, M. (2008). Value added learning. *Peer Review, 10*, 34–36.

Darling, C. A., Fleming, W. M., & Cassidy, D. (2009). The professionalization of family life education: Defining the field. *Family Relations, 59*, 330–345.

Donnelly-Smith, L. (2010). Making the most out of internships: An interview with Christi M. Pedra, senior vice-president for strategic new business development and marketing, Siemens Healthcare. *Peer Review, 12,* 9–11.

Evans, C., & Mori, C. (2005). Web-based diaries—Windows to student internship feedback. *Medical Education, 39,* 1169–1170.

Eyler, J. (2009). The power of experiential education. *Liberal Education, 95,* 24–31.

Jaschik, S. (2010, August 17). The satisfaction gap. *Inside Higher Education.* Retrieved from http://www.insidehighered.com/news/2010/08/17/asa#ixzz2TrKP8sCy

Kuh, G. (2008). *High-impact educational practices: What they are, who has access to them, and why they matter.* Washington, DC: Association of American Colleges and Universities.

McNair, T. B., & Albertine, S. (2012). Seeking high quality, high impact learning: The imperative of faculty development and curricular intentionality. *Peer Review, 14*(3), 4–5.

Mirrer, K. (2010). Designing new technologies to expand knowledge and information sharing in internship and experiential learning settings. *The International Journal of Technology, Knowledge and Society, 6*(4), 121–135.

O'Neill, N. (2010). Internships as high-impact practice: Some reflections on quality. *Peer Review, 12*(4), 4–8.

Steinberg, L. (2010). *Adolescence* (9th ed.). New York, NY: McGraw-Hill.

Thornton Moore, D. (2010). Forms and issues in experiential learning. *New Directions for Teaching and Learning, 124,* 3–13.

CHAPTER 3

The Professional Sequence and High-Impact Teaching: The Introductory Course

Deborah C. Bailey and Kimberly Tate

3.1 Overview

This chapter explains the implementation of several high-impact practices built into the introductory field experience course within our Family Studies' three-course professional sequence. It will explain how field work, experiential activities, structured journaling, and work group learning communities, are high-impact learning experiences that initiate our Family Studies students into the field of human services.

3.2 Course Design

The Family Studies major at Central Michigan University is designed to assist students with understanding the professional component of the major by introducing them to the skills and methods used for designing and implementing family life education programs and family case management. Our faculty designed the curriculum for the major with a commitment to active learning using high-impact practices. Borrowing Kuh's (2008) philosophy of high-impact practices, our courses are designed

---

D.C. Bailey (✉) • K. Tate
Human Development and Family Studies, Central Michigan University,
Mt Pleasant, MI, USA

with the belief that student development is shaped by many events across educational experiences in college and extends beyond the classroom and into the arena of field experiences. To this goal, we structured a three-course sequence designed to promote deep-level learning by providing structured experiences of field work, skill development, and a capstone internship that demands time, commitment, and full engagement from the students (Brower, 2013; Millis, 2012).

The sequence of three courses begins with a semester introduction to the professions served by the Human Development and Family Studies degrees (HDF 219 Field Work), followed by a semester of training in the skills and methods of interviewing assessment and programming (HDF 319 Skills and Methods), and then concludes with an internship semester focusing on applying family life education skills, methods, and theory while fulfilling an internship with a human service agency (HDF 419 Internship). This chapter explains the introduction to this professional sequence and the implementation of high-impact practices that aids students in clarification of their career goals while focusing on the development of helping skills. The key high-impact practices that we use for the Field Work course will be identified and followed with an explanation of practice. The chapter ends with identification of two challenges that we encounter with high-impact practices and steps taken to resolve these problems.

3.2.1 Activities That Have Applications to Settings On/Off Campus

The importance of making class work applicable to the experiences students will have in the field is essential. Brower (2013) identified the importance of intertwining classroom knowledge with real-world practice and explained that out-of-class opportunities increases student interest and engagement and improves learning. The weaving of knowledge and practice makes learning meaningful and creates a depth that cannot be achieved with traditional classroom instruction. A challenge to this practice is class size. Our course has up to 65 students each semester and is facilitated by one tenured faculty and three upper-class-level student assistants. This large class is subdivided into work groups of five students where, over time, they form a learning community that will support safe spaces for critical self-reflection, deconstruction, and application of course concepts for problem solving and case study analysis (Millis, 2012).

Students are required to complete 60 hours of field experience across one or two human service agencies while attending a two-hour weekly seminar, completing readings, journal entries, and case management activities. Students are exposed to the diverse nature of needs and programs in the human service industry through volunteer work and the opportunity to participate in a series of professional development experiences (Klien & Weiss, 2011). These opportunities include a poverty simulation, emergency mental health training, and the leadership service with the Family, Community, and Career Middle and High School conference.

Weekly seminars are designed to initiate thought with a brief introductory lecture that summarizes the readings while presenting a key theme in the practice of human services. As identified in the Report on High-Impact Educational Practices (Kuh, 2008), colleges need to provide curricula that meet the demands of future employers by challenging students to examine course concepts with real-world applications. This is done in the Field Work course by selecting themes that emphasize the character of the professional, professional ethics, skills, family life education, and focusing on services to groups in need. Since students take this course after successfully completing at least one of the Family Studies core courses, they come into the class with foundational knowledge of families and human development. This knowledge is linked to the mini-lectures requiring the students to integrate previous learning with practice.

This leads into application where the work groups are assigned a scenario designed to allow the students to explore the key elements of the evening topic. The groups are given guidelines and a time limit with expectations of sharing their work. Sometimes the work is shared in large group and sometimes it is posted on the course discussion board. Many times the groups are also charged with searching the web for news stories that align with the problem(s) plaguing their case studies.

3.2.2 Frequent Performance Feedback

Frequent performance feedback is considered essential for connecting with students and providing direction. Kuh (2008) explains that connecting with students aids in retention and engagement while Millis (2012) identifies the higher levels of learning through metacognition that come from encouraging students to think about what they are learning (Millis, 2012). There are several essential elements to this course which we connect with students by giving them performance feedback and encouraging them to think about how they are learning. Key learning objectives for this first course include knowledge of the career possibilities for having a Family Studies or Child Development major while understanding the needs of the diverse populations served. Through guided readings and weekly self-reflection journaling, the students come to recognize the challenges of working with those different from themselves and the skills needed to be effective human service professionals. The weekly journals provide students with the opportunity to think critically and uncover hidden beliefs and examine how they came to think and believe as they do. With structured questions to initiate the thinking in relation to the readings, class activity, and their experiences in the field, students complete entries of 350+ words. The course instructor reads a rotating selection of journals each week and with a team of senior-level class assistants aiding in reading and providing feedback. This ensures that every entry is read each week and all (students) involved feel heard, validated, challenged, and respected. This helps with providing a reciprocal sense of connection with faculty and students while increasing student confidence in their understanding.

3.2.3 Students Experience Diversity Through Contact with People Different from Themselves

The many individuals and families that our students will work with upon graduation will most likely come from diverse populations. The ability to work with and understand the needs of a diverse population was identified by Kuh (2008) as an essential learning outcome that may not be fully realized in a classroom. Accordingly, high-impact practices can aid student learning when coupled with diversity experiences (Davis, 2009; Kuh, 2008). The Field Work is our introductory course to the profession of human service where we strive to introduce students to diversity in the field as well as within the classroom. Students come into contact with people different from themselves through the field hours they complete at two human service agencies. Many of the students work 10+ hours at the community Soup Kitchen and Community Food Distribution program. These are paired with fieldwork with DHS Protective Services, Community Mental Health, and Community Senior Services. Their experiences with special needs populations are discussed in their small groups and written about in their journal throughout the semester. Though these are good experiences, we strive to find ways for the students to go deeper into a culture that is different from their own.

The Human Development and Family Studies Area sponsors a Poverty Simulation for the Field Work students. DeLashmutt and Rankin (2005) identified the value of the experience with helping nursing students to understand the challenges of poverty in a manner they may not ever know. Students from the Field Work class are invited to a Friday morning workshop to assume the role of an individual within a family struggling with the challenges of poverty. Upper-level students from the capstone Family Studies course assume roles of community agencies and businesses as service providers. Ideally these are students who have participated in the poverty workshops previously in their entry-level class. It is expected that all students participate in two separate poverty simulations during their course of studies in the major providing them with the unique range of experiences. First, students will take on a role of an individual in poverty, such as a homeless veteran or a single mother of three, while completing tasks and facing challenges representative of what a typical individual or family in poverty would face throughout a month. This poverty immersion experience teaches students compassion toward those in poverty and can reduce stigma toward this unique population (Patterson & Hulton, 2011). During their second poverty simulation as upper-level students, they facilitate the poverty simulation and act in a variety of roles (i.e. police officer, food pantry worker, employer, bank/loan collector, childcare worker). In these positions, students learn difficulties faced by human service professionals when resources needed exceed resources available.

At the conclusion of the simulation, there is a debriefing in which the student participants discuss frustrations and insights. Cranton (2002) frequently identifies the importance of building critical self-reflection into class activities and requirements as being essential for students to clarify what they are learning. This is followed by self-reflections that are designed to evoke responses allowing them to project the simulation experience to the realities of what they are seeing in their field sites (Vandsburger, Duncan-Datson, Akerson, & Dillion, 2010). Additional questions are asked to show students increase in understanding while building confidence with personal growth. Individuals currently working as human service professionals in the community are present during the debriefing and able to provide additional insight as to how experiences in the simulation translate in the real world.

3.2.4 Considerable Time Spent on Meaningful Tasks

Brower (2013) identifies the importance of designing curriculum and course instruction to encompass opportunities for meaningful tasks that require the students to engage in the application of knowledge to practice. Though there are many class activities, fieldwork experiences, and assignments that support the concept of engaging students in meaningful tasks, we have worked with our community agencies to provide the students with professional development opportunities where faculty accompany students with off-campus professional training or service in ways that will contribute to the development of their professional portfolio.

A professional training opportunity is offered to the students in collaboration with Community Mental Health. Students are invited to partake in a two-day, Mental Health First Aid Training. Facilitators from Community Mental Health train the students in recognizing and responding appropriately to a variety of mental health emergency situations including: anxiety disorders, depression, substance abuse, eating disorders, psychosis, and suicidal behaviors. According to Sander (2013), there is an increased need for dispelling the stigma related to mental illness and few people understand how to help those having problems. With so many students coming to campus with either histories or experiences of mental illness episodes, this training provides them with specific skills that increase their sense of efficacy for working with others. Students are first taught how to recognize each disorder listed above and learn a five-step action plan for responding. Referred to as ALGEE, these steps include: assess for risk of suicide or harm to self or others, listen nonjudgmentally, give reassurance and information, encourage appropriate professional help, and encourage self-help or other support strategies (Mental Health First Aid USA, n.d.). Upon completion, as certified first responders, students are able to recognize crisis and seek immediate help if they perceive the individual in crisis to be an immediate threat. If no immediate threat is perceived, students are equipped with the skills necessary to calm the individual and build rapport through nonjudgmental listening and reassuring the individual that they are not the first person to go through this, they can get help, and it will get better. Additionally, students are familiarized with formal and informal support systems, and how to find them in various geographic locations to help an individual receive needed services. Faculty participate in training with the students, creating opportunities for personal connections outside of class.

A third professional development activity is provided through the Michigan Family, Career, and Community Leaders of America, State Conference. Students participate as competition judges or workshop facilitators while working with Middle and High School students from across the state. This activity requires the Family Studies students to integrate academic knowledge of family and consumer science to the practice of teaching while giving insight into what it is they have learned from their own coursework. For many of the Field Work students, this one-day event gives them practical experience for working with adolescents with topics ranging from decision-making, career choices, violence, and interpersonal relations.

3.2.5 *Challenges to High-Impact Practices*

Each of these professional development activities extends beyond the required meeting days and times of class and the fieldwork. Though you may think getting students to volunteer time beyond grading requirements would be the greatest challenge, they are in fact identified by the students as being highly desirable. Instead, the most frequent challenges to the course are the critical self-reflections and work group assignments. It is not unusual for students to ask for more lectures and less case analysis or to express frustration with needing to write 350+ words in their journals. As Fox and Hackerman (2003) found in their study of faculty experience with using high-impact teaching strategies, students complain of not understanding the requirements of some activities and prefer the comfort of highly polished skills of memorization with no critical thought or application.

To increase student engagement with the journal entries, two support strategies appear to help. First, all weekly journal questions are provided to the students at the start of the semester and discussed during the first class. The instructor provides explanation as to the purpose of the journal as initiating personal reflection with the need to think deeply and write lots. An example of a well-written entry from a previous semester is provided with students having ready access to everything through a Black Board Folder. Then, the journal questions are introduced during the weekly sessions as part of the content knowledge where at the end of class, students are given 5–15 minutes to start writing. This has shown to increase and improve critical thought as well as expand individual understanding of the class reading and activity.

The second support strategy is the use of upper-level students as instructional assistants for class meetings and reading journal entries. A team of three senior- or graduate-level students work as aids with the Field Work course and are provided with a small stipend. Each member of the team is assigned four learning community work groups. The instructional aids meet with the professor each week to prepare for the upcoming class by working through the activity and to discuss any emerging concerns or needs of the students. During class, the instructional aids spend time with each of their four work groups encouraging discussion and answering questions while ensuring all of the students in class are engaged and on-task. This enables the course instructor to facilitate learning for the large class and more freely circulate around the room. The instructional aides also assist by reading the weekly journal entries for their groups and noting each week which student journals are being read by faculty and flagging entries needing additional attention. The assistance of the instructional aids provides needed support for the students by providing an essential link of personal experience with attention.

In conclusion, the work we do in the Field Work course lays the foundation to the Skills and Methods course that follows. These courses prepare students for the Internship experience of the third course of the professional sequence. The value of the sequences is ultimately seen in the increased knowledge the students have about professional career options but also in a strong sense of efficacy in choosing what they want to focus on in the remaining year of their university education.

References

Brower, A. (2013). High impact educational practices at University of Wisconsin, Madison. Retrieved from http://tle.wisc.edu/node/1034

Cranton, P. (2002). Teaching for transformation. In J. M. Ross-Gordon (Ed.), *New directions for adult and continuing education, No. 93: Contemporary viewpoints on teaching adults effectively* (pp. 63–71). San Francisco, CA: Jossey-Bass.

Davis, T. S. (2009). Diversity practice in social work: Examining theory in practice. *Journal of Ethnic & Cultural Diversity in Social Work, 18*(40), 40–69. doi:10.1080/1531320090287/461.

DeLashmutt, M. B., & Rankin, E. A. (2005). A different kind of clinical experience: Poverty up close and personal. *Nurse Educator, 30*(4), 143–149.

Fox, M. A., & Hackerman, N. (2003). *Evaluating and improving undergraduate teaching in science, technology, engineering, and mathematics.* Washington, DC: The National Academies Press.

Klien, M., & Weiss, F. (2011). Is forcing them worth the effort? Benefits of mandatory internships for graduates from diverse family backgrounds and labour market entry. *Studies in Higher Education, 36*(8), 969–987.

Kuh, G. D. (2008). *High-impact educational practices: What they are, who has access to them, and why they matter.* Washington, DC: Association of American Colleges and Universities.

Mental Health First Aid USA. (n.d.). First aid strategies. Retrieved from http://www.mentalhealthfirstaid.org/cs/first_aid:strategies

Millis, B. J. (2012). Active learning strategies in face-to-face classes. IDEA Paper No. 53. Retrieved from http://www.theideacenter.org/sites/default/files/paperidea_53.pdf

Patterson, N., & Hulton, L. J. (2011). Enhancing nursing student's understanding of poverty through simulation. *Public Health Nursing, 20*(2), 143–151. doi:10.1111/j.1525-1446.2011.00999x.

Sander, L. (2013). Holistic mental health-care can earn colleges a new accolade. *The Chronicle of Higher Education*, (Newsletter). Retrieved from http://chronicle.com/article/Holistic-Mental-Health-Care/139285/

Vandsburger, E., Duncan-Datson, R., Akerson, E., & Dillion, T. (2010). The effects of poverty simulation, an experiential learning modality, on students' understanding of life in poverty. *Journal of Teaching in Social Work, 30*(3), 300–316.

Supplemental Sources

Stage, F. K., Muller, P. A., Kinzie, J., & Simmons, A. (1998). *Creating learner centered classrooms: What does learning theory have to say?* Washington, DC: Clearinghouse on Higher Education and the Association for the Study of Higher Education.

Weimer, M. (2002). *Learner-centered teaching: Five key changes to practice.* San Francisco: Jossey-Bass.

CHAPTER 4

The Professional Sequence and High-Impact Teaching: Skills, Methods, and Internships

Edgar C.J. Long and Deborah C. Bailey

4.1 Overview

All students majoring in Family Studies at Central Michigan University are required to take a three-course sequence designed to teach fundamental skills for family life educators and gain practice using these skills during an internship in a human service agency. The professional course sequence is HDF 219 Field Work, HDF 319 Skills and Methods in Human Development and Family Studies, and HDF 419 Human Development and Family Studies Internship. The Field Work course introduces students to the professional practices most commonly associated with Family Studies majors. A detailed discussion of the course is provided in Chap. 3 so it will not be discussed here. It should be noted that the importance of student engagement for connecting theory to practice is the guiding philosophy for the three-course sequence as Family Studies students often struggle with understanding how the courses they so enjoy will lead them to a paying job (Bailey, 2010). The three-course professional sequence came out of a faculty commitment to preparing students to become professionals who would be ready to leave the classroom and find jobs upon graduation.

E.C.J. Long (✉) • D.C. Bailey
Human Development and Family Studies, Central Michigan University, Mt Pleasant, MI, USA

The first part of this chapter will share how the Skills and Methods course focuses on skill development. The final part of the chapter will describe the three-course sequence culminating in the Internship course. This chapter will explain the relationship between high-impact practices with the development of professional skills. Specifically it will address high-impact practices including, spending considerable amounts of time on meaningful tasks, faculty and student peers interacting about substantive matters, students experiencing diversity through contact with people who are different than themselves, students receiving frequent performance feedback, activities that have applications to different settings on/off campus, and authentic connections with peers, faculty, community, and/or the university.

4.2 HIGH-IMPACT PRACTICES

4.2.1 *Faculty and Student Peers Interact About Substantive Matters*

Knowledge comes from a dialectical process that invites students to a deeper level of learning and happens through multiple discussions with peers and faculty (Kuh, 2008). Students work with smaller amounts of information but explore it in detail. Instruction of the Skills and Methods course focuses on the skills of interviewing and program development, and uses high-impact practices focus on student's depth of knowledge and abilities.

The first part of the course uses Young's (2013) *Learning the Art of Helping* to introduce students to the skill of interviewing, a precursor for counseling. This provides the students with a structural outline of practice for interviewing skills and family life education. Students read, discuss, and apply the essential skills deemed important for entry-level human service professionals (Hall, Gibbe, & Lubman, 2012). Students' video record and compare their own interviewing and helping skills with those of their peers "before and after." The before taping precedes assigned reading and class discussions, while the after taping follows several weeks of reading, discussing, and practicing. The pre-and-post assessments are student lead, evaluating and supporting each other while identifying growth areas needing more improvement. Though the course process is faculty led, the learning is individualized. In contrast to other classes in the major, the Skills and Methods class has a limit of 25 students per section. This allows faculty opportunities to know the students and provide meaningful feedback through observation and reflective writings. During the semester, there is a goal that students develop a sense of trust among their class members, as much of the learning is done in small groups. Trust and comfort with peers is necessary as the interviewing portion of the course can evoke uncomfortable emotions and insecurities (Millis, 2012). Students are vulnerable as they practice reflective listening and begin to identify feelings and meanings associated with a fellow classmates' communication. Videotaping sessions are challenging, students often express embarrassment recording and listening to themselves. However, they are pleasantly surprised as they evaluate their skill improvement across time. As one student wrote in her personal reflection,

> I hated recording myself! That first week was awful. I didn't know what I was doing and was annoyed that we didn't get much direction. But after a few weeks of reading and practicing, I can see a big difference! I guess if we had more direction it would have changed what I did and I wouldn't see how much I have learned.

Another student wrote,

> I can see how I am learning some counseling techniques. First off I can say that my body language is so much better. When I compare my first taping with this last one it is apparent how important it is to be attentive in how you sit and listen. I think that I am listening better and I didn't even know that I wasn't [listening] before.

4.2.2   *Activities Have Application On and Off Campus*

In past semesters, we have heard students comment that the information they learn in the classroom has little to no application to the real world. Accordingly, Kuh (2008) identified the need to practice integrative and applied learning that helps students utilize knowledge that they have identified as being important and useful in their future work. The Skills and Methods course helps students recognize the relevancy of course readings, and classroom activities provide them with opportunities to practice family life education through program development. Though we recognize the relevance of Kuh's work, we still teach and rely on a couple of textbooks that provide students with information we believe is essential. The second part of the Skills and Methods course uses Powell and Cassidy's textbook, *Family Life Education* (2007), and initiates the class to the career work of family life education programming. At this juncture, we are not looking for course content but emphasize the preventative and remedial model of family life education programming, using a strengths-based perspective (Doherty, 1995; Duncan & Goddard, 2010). In small groups, students are challenged as they develop a family systems-based program, utilizing theories and concepts from previous coursework. The creation of a family life education program follows a grant development model with the initiation of a prospectus in connection to a Request for Proposals. Students learn the essentials of following instructions and begin learning the concise writing skills that Dustin, Craigen, and Milliken (2010) identified as being essential for human service graduates. Students design programs based on a needs assessment and finally implement formative and summative evaluation processes. A two-to-three-page leader's guide is created to demonstrate how the student understands key principles of best practice in program development. Finally, students write a program reflection, evaluating the challenges they faced, the practicality of their program, and any challenges they foresee in the implementation of the program and evaluation. The usefulness of this activity is frequently mentioned in the internship course as students are asked to demonstrate some aspect of family life education for the agency where they are working. For some students, this becomes an opportunity to create a program, facilitate a learning group, or assist with program evaluation or grant development. In one instance, a student created and implemented a workshop for first generation college students' parents during the University summer orientation. Parents were given information about the challenges and benefits of a college education and what they could do to enable a successful transition for their students. Another student designed a parenting class for adolescent mothers and was able to implement it on her Native American Reservation.

The challenges of the Skills and Methods course comes from student anxiety as the demands for critical thinking and deep learning often exceed anything they have experienced. Students must earn a minimum grade of C+ before taking the Internship. Though grades are important, bending and shaping is more important with special detail being given to not breaking spirits. Teaching strategies are anything but lecture making, each class meeting is different. The role of faculty is helping students develop the skills necessary for working with individuals and families. Much of this work is done through the use of case study analyses, community scavenger hunts, internet media reports, and group facilitation and team-building activities. In addition, students share in the responsibilities of designing and implementing class meetings, their needs dictate the agenda and structure of the class meetings. Sharing the responsibility for class content and activities encourages faculty to take the focus off of themselves (Millis, 2012), getting students engaged in instruction within the class. This pedagogy fits well with the class where the students determine what they will read and what will be moved forward into the realms of practice.

4.2.3 *Authentic Connections Made with Peers, Faculty, and Community*

The third course in the family studies professionals sequence is the Internship. Our Internship course is designed to come at the end of the students' coursework in the major so they can integrate experience with knowledge, and practice the skills needed for human service professions. The premise of the Internship course is based on making authentic connections with peers, faculty, and community. This learning paradigm (Barr & Tagg, 1995) looks beyond the instructor, creating student learning activities and cultivating connections with faculty, peers, and the community. This encourages greater student engagement and expands the realm of resources useful for equipping students for professional roles. Making the world the classroom assists students in getting a job in the real world. It is impossible to teach students everything they need to know to get a job in the real world unless we make that world the classroom.

For many of our students, the internship experience is pivotal to their successful transition from student to professional. It comes at the end of their coursework culminating in an intellectual, emotional, academic, and professional experience that for many is the highlight of their undergraduate education (Sweitzer & King, 2014). The process of securing their internship site forces them to contact agencies in a variety of communities in the same way they would when applying for a job.

Some of our students go straight from undergraduate studies to graduate school as they pursue careers as marriage and family therapists, social workers, or psychologists. A few will go on to doctoral work in research and teaching, but many are simply looking forward to wrapping up there education and progressing to a career. Therefore, the internship serves as the medium by which they will become professionals. Students find their own worksites and interview with potential supervisors. Since their worksites must be secured before they can register for the Internship, they immediately start networking with friends and calling agencies.

In contrast to the research of Klien and Weiss (2011), where they found that mandatory internships did not contribute to positive employment outcomes for many students from lower-income families, we have found internships to be the difference between students who get jobs in the field and those who do not. Over the years, we have witnessed our graduates who had internships with the Department of Human Services, or other human service agencies, network themselves into the kinds of work they had hoped for because of the connections they have made with peers in the field. Overall, about 15 % of our students are offered jobs at their internship sites each year.

The internship is directly shaped by the student-constructed learning objectives that reflect the goals of Family Life Education, the personal and professional interests of the students, and the needs of the agency. Objectives are written with the cooperation of their site supervisors and later discussed in their learning reflections. Students write weekly entries in their electronic journals, describing their thoughts about their experiences in the field. They focus on many things but often deal with their feelings, about themselves, clients, situations, their colleagues or supervisors. The faculty supervisor reads the journals and makes comments or asks questions, helping the student think more deeply about their experiences in light of their past courses and future career aspirations. This type of feedback often has a personal quality that is not typical of student-faculty interaction and thus is a new experience for students. This kind of attention is possible by the smaller number of students in each section of the field experience course. Numbers can range from 15 students or less during the fall semesters to 25 students to a section during the spring and summer.

Four times during the semester, the students meet on campus if they are in close proximity to the University. The campus meetings are discussion seminars where the students share their experiences and practice networking skills. This environment helps students support and encourage each other while having time to talk to their faculty supervisor. Throughout the semester, the faculty supervisor visits students at least once at their worksites. This builds relationships and creates strong bonds between the faculty, the student, and the sponsoring agencies.

4.2.4 Students Experience Diversity Through Contact with People Different from Themselves

Diversity has been identified by many in higher education as being essential preparation for undergraduates if they are to be successful in their professions. When students encounter diversity, they come to know themselves better and are better prepared to be authentic in their endeavors (Kuh, 2008). In this final section, we will discuss the challenges encountered with the Internship course and how high-impact practices help faculty encourage students to do more than they thought possible by encouraging them to work with agencies that provide opportunities for diversity.

Central Michigan University is located in the center of Michigan, and primarily attracts students from rural communities and smaller cities. Before coming to the University, many of our students have little exposure to economic, cultural, ethnic, racial, sexual orientation, or religious diversity. This particular university is a homogenous group; more than 80 % of the students are Euro-American. However, for many of the students, this is the most diverse experience of their lives. Work in the human services field often involves diverse groups of people; therefore, it is imperative that students have experiences with minority populations.

The Internship course provides many of our students with their first opportunity to work with minority groups. Students are encouraged to take their internships in settings where they can interact with groups of people they would not normally work with. Many students live on or near campus and do not have the time or the transportation to visit urban areas in the state where there is significantly more diversity. Therefore, we encourage them to pair their internship with the summer term or at the end of their campus education so they can travel. The limited number of potential internship sites near the University makes it challenging for all our students to secure really good internships near campus. As with most rural college towns, our student population exceeds the number of people in the town itself. Local human service agencies are fewer in number and flooded with requests from students in other disciplines looking for field experience worksites. Ultimately, our urging and support of diversity experiences is a key element of their internship that is met with both excitement and hesitancy.

For those who accept the challenge, the true value of working with a diverse population becomes visible in their journal entries. As they encounter clients, coworkers, and communities different from themselves, they write about it in words that describe anger, frustration, fear, anxiety, and confusion. Here faculty probes and feedback encourage students to think more deeply about what is being felt and said. An example of this feedback is best illustrated with a specific example of a student who wrote about being angry with a mother who chose drug use over parenting her young child. The faculty advisor wrote, "Your anger and frustration with this parent who is addicted to drugs is understandable. However, your anger is in no way helpful for you or the client. You have an issue with your anger towards this woman and you need to work on that anger." It is very common for a parent who is addicted to substances to display poor parenting skills. However, the intern may need to clearly hear that the problem is not the mother; the problem is with her own response to the mother. The feedback is meant to be constructive, to challenge students to work on their perceptions of blame and frustration with the realities of work in this field. The opportunities of working with a diverse population allow these beliefs to surface and give students opportunities to understand the strengths and weaknesses they bring to the clients. This very personal faculty student exchange best takes place with the guidance of faculty supervisors who have built relationships with the students through site visits, on-campus seminars, electronic journals, and previous coursework.

Conclusion

The creation of the three-course sequence evolved slowly over the years through a variety of processes and it continues to evolve. The Family Studies faculty have always been concerned with the employment outcomes for our students and been attentive to identifying and meeting the needs of both students and human service agencies in Mid- and Northern Michigan. Student learning is limited if we focus solely on teaching theory and content. We believe the internship is essential for professional success, helping students understand the reality of current and future work in this field. Jobs our students will have tomorrow may not currently exist. However, the use of high-impact practices equips students with the knowledge and skills necessary for retooling in a work environment that is ever changing.

References

Bailey, D. C. (2010). Engaging family studies students: Using a self-narrative to improve one's teaching. *Family Science Review, 15*(1), 31–39.

Barr, R. B., & Tagg, J. (1995). From teaching to learning: A new paradigm for undergraduate education. *Change, 27*(6), 12–23.

Doherty, W. J. (1995). Boundaries between parent and family education and family therapy. *Family Relations, 44,* 353–358.

Duncan, S. F., & Goddard, H. W. (2010). *Family life education: Principles and practices for effective outreach.* Thousand Oaks, CA: Sage Publications.

Dustin, J. C., Craigen, L., & Milliken, T. (2010). Who or whom? A program innovation to improve the writing skills of human service students. *Journal of Human Services, 30*(1), 66–71.

Hall, K., Gibbe, T., & Lubman, D. I. (2012). Motivational interviewing techniques: Facilitating behavioral change in the general practice setting. *Australian Family Physician, 41*(9).

Klien, M., & Weiss, F. (2011). Is forcing them worth the effort? Benefits of mandatory internships for graduates from diverse family backgrounds at labor market entry. *Studies in Higher Education, 36*(8), 969–987. doi:10.1080/03075079.2010.487936.

Kuh, G.D. (2008). *High-impact educational practices: What they are, who has access to them, and why they matter.* Washington, DC: Association of American Colleges and Universities..

Millis, B. J. (2012). Active learning strategies in face-to-face classes. IDEA Paper No. 53. Retrieved from http://www.theideacenter.org/sites/default/files/paperidea_53.pdf

Powell, L. H., & Cassidy, D. (2007). *Family life education: An introduction* (2nd ed.). Mountain View, CA: Mayfield Publishing.

Sweitzer, H. F., & King, M. A. (2014). *The successful internship: Personal, professional, and individual development in experiential learning* (4th ed.). Belmont, CA: Brooks/Cole.

Young, M.E. (2013). *Learning the art of helping: Building blocks and techniques* (5th ed.). New York, NY: Pearson.

Supplemental Sources

Arcus, M. E., Schvaneveldt, J., & Moss, J. (1993). *Handbook of family life education: Foundations of family life education* (Vol. 1). Newbury Park, CA: Sage Publications.

Astin, A. W. (1984). Student involvement: A developmental theory for higher education. *Journal of College Student Personnel, 25*, 297–308.

Darling, C. A., Fleming, W. M., & Cassidy, D. (2009). Professionalization of family life education: Defining the field. *Family Relations, 58*, 330–345.

Harris, V. W., Chartier, K., & Davis, E. (2010). A start to finish teaching model for education courses. *Family Science Review, 15*(2), 15–23.

McNeil, R. C. (2001). A program evaluation model: Using Bloom's taxonomy to identify outcome indicators in outcomes-based program evaluations. *Journal of Adult Education, 40*(2), 24–29.

Myers-Walls, J. A., Ballard, S. M., Darling, C. A., & Myers-Bowman, K. S. (2011). Reconceptualizing the domain and boundaries of family life education. *Family Relations, 60*, 357–372. doi: 10.111/j.1741-3729.2011.00659.x

CHAPTER 5

Personal and Professional Development Through Internship Engagement

Maria K. Schmidt

5.1 Introduction

Experiential education has been an integral part of human history, beginning in ancient communities with the need to survive, and continuing to the twenty-first century need to develop and enhance skills for success as a professional. In previous centuries, children were taught vocational skills by parents. When children became interested in other vocations, apprenticeship programs began (Woodward et al., 2012). Continuing in this tradition, universities are providing students with opportunities to gain personal and professional skills through civic engagement (Sweitzer & King, 2009).

The Human Development and Family Studies (HDFS) program and Youth Development (YD) program at Indiana University have taken seriously the need for students to have experiential learning opportunities. Our department determined that there was a need to assist students in making the connection between college studies and careers though high-impact learning practices (Kuh, 2008). An academic internship was seen as a vital component of the student's success upon graduation and was incorporated into the curriculum.

M.K. Schmidt (✉)
Applied Health Science, Indiana University, Bloomington, IN, USA

Creating and growing the internship program has been a successful experience for our students and faculty. This chapter will describe the implementation and academic requirements of our internship program as well as the decision to add a pre-internship experience in the form of service-learning to our professional preparation course. The concluding thoughts will discuss the challenges and successes of implementing these programs.

5.2 Implementation of Civic Engagement—Internships

Human Development and Family Studies majors are prepared to function professionally in a variety of settings through university courses and practical experiences. The primary purpose of the internship program is to provide experiential learning outside of the academic setting, where students gain vital skills and experience (Kuh, 2008). Through these experiences, students sample potential specialties, explore workplace culture, and gain experience. In addition, internships enable students to develop a network of professional relationships that are useful when seeking employment after graduation.

5.2.1 Contact with Diverse Populations

The internship provides students with hands-on experience in community programs serving individuals within specific stages of life such as childhood, adolescence, adulthood, or older age. Specialties for HDFS/YD professionals might also include issues such as sexuality, spirituality, health and wellness, adoption, family law, family policy, family life education, therapy, counseling, fatherhood, poverty, and immigrants, to name a few.

Many students choose placements in their hometowns or other locations away from the university community. Students choose to work in a variety of sites including child care, youth services, boys and girls clubs, homeless shelters, and elder care or with projects and program development within the agency. The diversity and global element of high-impact learning is implemented in our program as students are encouraged, and most often choose to complete internships in community agencies which offer experiences with individuals who are different from themselves, including interning abroad (Kuh, 2008).

The internship allows students to apply their knowledge and skills in a real-life situation, and to develop professional experience in a structured, nurturing environment (Kuh, 2008). As students continue to develop their professional skills, they gain a better understanding of the issues and problems they will face as a human service professional on the job. During the internship, students become a part of the agency (paid or unpaid) and are expected to conduct themselves in a professional manner while learning from their experiences.

5.2.2 Building Relationships Through Authentic Connection

The objective of the HDFS/YD internship program at Indiana University is to provide students with professional experience through high-impact learning. A common element of high-impact learning is for students to build relationships and interact with others over an extended period of time to gain valuable insight through mentoring (Kuh, 2008). To achieve this element, our internship goals for students include:

- observing and working alongside dedicated professionals in the field, to understand professional practice, including professional ethics;
- working independently and with colleagues;
- applying professional knowledge and skills; and
- developing networks and contacts.

It is also our goal that students are able to apply academic knowledge, which is another high-impact learning element, through:

- applying theories and research from human and family development disciplines to the challenges facing individuals and families; and
- applying concepts and skills gained from academic experience to a professional work setting.

In addition, the internship is an opportunity for students to hone their personal character development, and reflect on the person they are becoming, another high-impact element of practice (Felten & Clayton, 2011; Kuh, 2008). We hope that students acquire professional work experience to further develop and integrate personal characteristics (e.g., self-awareness and emotional stability, interpersonal and group process skills, communication, collaboration and teaching skills, problem-solving skills, cultural competence, knowledge of community support services, and professional ethics and behavior).

5.2.3 *Time Spent on Meaningful Tasks*

Internship in Human Development and Family Studies is a six-credit-hour course of professional development toward the undergraduate degree. The six credits require each student to work 270 hours in the chosen agency. Students receive a grade of **S**atisfactory or **F**ailure for this course. The internship must last a minimum of nine weeks and maximum of 16 weeks. Due to the intensity and time commitment of the internship, it is strongly suggested that the intern not take other classes or have significant commitments during the internship experience. Interns may be paid or volunteer their time, depending upon the resources of the agency. Placement at a student's current place of employment is not recommended. However, if a student requests an internship placement at her/his current place of employment, internship activities must be separate and substantially different from the regular duties and work hours. The boundaries between regular work activity and internship tasks must be clearly spelled out in agreements between the intern, site supervisor, and faculty advisor.

5.3 ACADEMIC REQUIREMENTS FOR THE INTERNSHIP PROGRAM

The internship experience at Indiana University for the HDFS/YD majors is designed to be completed after the student's junior year. Prior to completing the internship requirement, students must meet academic eligibility requirements. Students are required to attend an *Orientation Meeting* with the HDFS Internship Coordinator in their sophomore year to obtain forms and information regarding internships. At this meeting, students complete an *Internship Application Card* noting their contact information, anticipated semester of completing the internship requirement, GPA and academic eligibility. Academic eligibility includes the following prerequisites:

- successful completion of 18 hours of HDFS/YD courses, and completion of the development course (childhood, adolescence, adult) that corresponds to the age group with which she/he will be working;

- successful completion of our *Professional Preparation for Human Development and Family Studies* course; and
- junior or senior academic standing, with an overall GPA of 2.5.

Students are responsible for securing an internship site with the assistance of their HDFS Internship Coordinator. Students are encouraged to select a site that will match well with their professional goals. As noted earlier, students are encouraged to choose as site which varies from their own experiences and provides diversity and growth.

5.3.1 Authorization Procedures

Once the agency approves the student's placement as an intern, students must complete authorization documentation and seek approval from the HDFS Internship Coordinator prior to registration and beginning their service in the agency. The forms include:

- *Internship Authorization Form*, available from the HDFS Internship Coordinator. This form must be completed prior to registration. This form is signed by the student and the HDFS Internship Coordinator and is submitted to the Dean's Office for authorization to register.
- The *Memorandum of Understanding* is the job description for the internship and is written as a summary of goals and objectives or learning experiences. In cooperation with the site supervisor, the student identifies tasks and responsibilities to be performed during the internship experience, establishing 3–5 learning objectives and goals, which are specific to the organization. The *Memorandum of Understanding* is submitted to the HDFS Internship Coordinator on agency letterhead, and (1) identifies the duration of the internship (dates), (2) includes the learning objectives and activities, and (3) is signed by the student and the site supervisor.
- *Statement of Justification* is a brief, one-page document, where students discuss how this internship experience and/or site will enhance her HDFS/YD curriculum. (e.g., Does it add to knowledge about an age group or issue? How does it fit with your career objective/goals? What are your personal and professional goals for your internship experience?)
- *Release from Liability* is available from the HDFS Internship Coordinator at the time of authorization.

Upon completion of the required forms, students schedule an appointment with the HDFS Internship Coordinator. The appointment involves the approval of the internship site and learning objectives. This approval process encompasses the HDFS Internship Coordinator reviewing the *Memorandum of Understanding* looking at the ways the student will experience diversity and growth within the setting, as well as the meaningful tasks in which the student will engage (Kuh, 2008). Once approved, students are eligible to register for the internship class and may begin counting their hours of experience.

5.4 Requirements for Completing the HDFS Internship

Professional conduct during the internship is important and students are reminded of issues such as dress, attitude, punctuality, dedication, ethical conduct, confidentiality, and notification to the agency if they cannot keep a time commitment. While in the field, students are encouraged to communicate regularly with their agency supervisor and are required to maintain a journal and time log to fulfill university requirements.

5.4.1 Reflection and Feedback

In the journals, students discuss their experiences and reflect on those experiences. Three journals are submitted to the HDFS Internship Coordinator:

- Journal 1 is due after 70 hours;
- Journal 2, at midterm, is due after 135 hours; and
- Journal 3 is due after 200 hours.

At the conclusion of the internship, and after the student has completed a minimum of 270 hours, a final paper is submitted to the HDFS Internship Coordinator. This paper is an overall reflection by the student of her/his experiences. The process of reflecting and receiving frequent feedback from the HDFS Internship Coordinator through journal entries and the final paper is a key component of our program and an element of high-impact learning (Kuh, 2008). The majority of the paper is a self-analysis which requires the student to discuss the following:

- positive/meaningful experiences;
- negative/frustrating experiences;
- personal and professional benefits of the internship;
- how the experience shaped the student's philosophy and approach to the profession;
- concerns or issues regarding the internship (e.g., policies, clients, the agency, the system);
- skills and theoretical knowledge acquired in academic preparation which were used in the internship experience; and
- specific situation(s) during the internship in which the student felt especially prepared as a result of previous coursework?

Students are also required to include the following appendices in their final paper:

- a signed log of hours;
- an exit interview with the site supervisor and the HDFS Internship Coordinator;
- a copy of the professional thank you note which the student sent to the site supervisor; and
- an updated résumé including the internship experience.

In accordance with the high-impact learning goals of providing the student with frequent and substantive feedback (Kuh, 2008), the site supervisor is asked to complete a midterm and final evaluation of the student, both of which are submitted to the HDFS Internship Coordinator.

While internships have been a remarkable addition to the HDFS/YD curriculum, the faculty realized that students were continually nearing the end of their coursework without having a full understanding of what they wanted to do upon graduation. This realization led to the implementation of service-learning as a bridge between theory and practice.

5.5 Implementation of Civic Engagement—Service-Learning

While teaching a professional preparation course, I noticed that students were completing their coursework with little opportunity for hands-on career-related experiences. Service-learning experiences enhance academic learning and vice versa (Kuh, 2008). Adding this component to the course curriculum was not so much about the "service" (i.e., understanding community needs) but rather about gaining hands-on experience to promote individual professional growth. I require students to engage in supervised service-learning as a component of the curriculum in a professional preparation course. Service-learning is also an option in a couple other courses, (e.g., Human Development I, where students are able to gain insight through interacting with young children and connecting theory to practice). The overall goals of the service-learning assignments are (1) to facilitate students' giving of themselves in a setting which is diverse from their normal realms of experience and (2) to enhance the learning of the course curriculum through their community service (Kuh, 2008).

Service-learning at Indiana University is well supported. Through our *Center for Innovative Teaching and Learning*, we have a well-staffed *Service-Learning Program* which supports faculty, students, and community partners. Through this program, students are able to connect with community partners. Students may also independently find a community agency in which to participate.

When I first began using service-learning, I chose to work directly with one agency. I met with the agency directors, and sent 50 HDFS students to them to complete 30 hours of service-learning. This became quite overwhelming for the agency, and we soon negotiated fewer hours for the students to complete. Overcoming the challenges and frustrations with trying to complete hours, the students reflected in their final journals that this was a very valuable experience and should remain a part of the curriculum.

In the years that have followed, I continue to work with specifically chosen community agencies, with more variety of options, and continue to send 45–65 students into the community to complete 30 hours of service-learning. Students may provide a direct service through volunteering or complete a project that benefits a community agency or organization. The students continue to experience frustrations, but most are caused by their own time management.

In their final journal reflections, students comment that service-learning is valuable to their overall college experience and life experiences.

> funny enough, even though it was what stressed me the most, service learning will leave a lasting impression with me. I loved every one of the kids that I worked with. I was able to actually witness them changing and developing

day by day. It was such a good experience to apply what I have been learning in school for the past three years. (Student *Final Self-Assessment* Assignment, 2012)

Another student noted that "(p)articipating in the service learning was a wonderful experience. The service learning experience really changed me as a person". (Student *Final Self-Assessment* Assignment, 2012)

Our program continues to support service-learning as an excellent component of our Professional Preparation course. However, we have learned that we must be mindful of how many hours of service-learning we require of our students during any given semester. There are challenges when students take multiple classes in the same semester which require service-learning as this is a significant time commitment on top of other classes and jobs. We currently have one class in which 30 hours of service-learning is required and two classes with 15 hours of service-learning as an optional assignment. When given the option to do service-learning, 75 percent of students choose it as a component of their curriculum. In final reflection journals, students stated they were pleased to "apply classroom knowledge to the service learning organization" (Student *Final Service-Learning Journal* Assignment, 2012). Students also noted, "What meant most to me throughout this entire course is the service-learning that I have had the chance to participate in" (Student *Final Service-Learning Journal* Assignment, 2012).

During service-learning, students are required to complete journal entries documenting their activities and experiences, and to reflect on those experiences (Kuh, 2008). Reflection sections of journal entries describe feelings, personal values, attitudes, and ethical issues related to the experience. This reflection section also includes observations of professionalism and career-related issues (e.g., honesty/integrity, reliability/responsibility, respect for others, compassion/empathy, self-awareness/knowledge of limits, communication/collaboration, altruism/advocacy). Students are also asked to describe their reactions to being at a site which differs from their personal experiences, or any shifts in attitude they experienced regarding professionalism. In classes where service-learning is optional, journals relate directly to the course content, (e.g., Human Development I students are asked to observe children's growth and development in all domains).

Students submit journals for grading after every ten hours of service. The final journal is more comprehensive and includes a log of hours signed by the site supervisor, an evaluation completed by the site supervisor, and a thank you note from the student to the agency expressing appreciation for helping the student complete course requirements. These components also feed into the high-impact element regarding rich and frequent feedback for students (Kuh, 2008).

In one of the final class meetings, students orally reflect on service-learning and how it connected with the course, professional goals, personal growth, and community needs (Felten & Clayton, 2011). This discussion is led by the course instructor and often develops into questions and comments related to course content and the students' future career goals.

> The parts of this class that impacted me the most were definitely...the service learning. Although it was a lot of work, I think the service learning definitely helped me become sure of my own career path and gave me much more practice working with young children. (Student *Final Self-Assessment* Assignment, 2012)

Our program has found that service-learning lends itself quite well as a bridge between students gaining academic and theoretical knowledge and being able to apply that knowledge in practical situations. Students make decisions about their service-learning such as whether it will involve a specific age group or a community issue with which they want to engage.

5.6 Concluding Thoughts

As we attempt to usher young adults from academic classroom work to professional work, the implementation of high-impact learning experiences in the form of an internship and service-learning into our HDFS/YD curriculum has proven to be beneficial to our program and to students. Upon graduation, students have a better idea of what they want to do. They have discovered the likes and dislikes of their chosen field. Students have been provided with an opportunity to connect with dedicated professionals and to develop networks and contacts. As a result, our program has grown as more students find jobs and experience success in graduate school.

Along the way, we have learned that communication with students and supervisors is critical. Letters of expectation are sent to internship and service-learning supervisors. For agencies with close ties to the university, partnerships have been established to decrease the burden on the agency and improve student success. The internship handbook and supplemental documents have served as a resource for outlining students' responsibilities in their career development and have aided in the communication between academic advisors, HDFS Internship Coordinators, and community agencies. Not all students take full advantage of the service-learning and internship program; some have an attitude of "just get the assignment done." However, for those students who take advantage of the service-learning and internship opportunities, success meets them at the open door.

References

Felten, P., & Clayton, P. H. (2011). Service-learning. *New Directions for Teaching and Learning, 124,* 75–84.

Kuh, G. D. (2008). High-impact educational practices: What they are, who has access to them, and why they matter. *American Association of Colleges and Universities.*

Sweitzer, H. F., & King, M. A. (2009). *The successful internship: Personal, professional, and civic development* (3rd ed.). California: Cengage Learning.

Woodward, E., Thornhill, J., True, M., O'Meara, M., Hayes, R., Demers, M., & Bentancourt, A. (2012). *Why internships are good: The best education money can't buy.* Charleston, SC: CreateSpace.

Supplemental Sources

Bravo, D., & Whiteley, C. (2005). *The internship advantage: Get real-world job experience to launch your career.* Upper Saddle River, NJ: Prentice Hall.

Chertavian, G. (2012). *A year up: How a pioneering program teaches young adults real skills for real jobs with real success.* New York: Viking.

Gerdes, L. (Ed.). (2011). *National service (Opposing Viewpoints).* New York: Greenhaven Press.

Molee, L. M., Henry, M. E., Sessa, V. I., & McKinney-Prupis, E. R. (2010). Assessing learning in service-learning courses through critical reflection. *Journal of Experiential Education, 33,* 239–257.

Perlin, R. (2011). *Intern nation: How to earn nothing and learn little in the brave new economy.* New York: Venso.

Schmidt, M. K., (2013). *Internship handbook guidelines and procedures: SPH-F497 Internship in Human Development and Family Studies.* 4th Ed. Bloomington, IN: Indiana University.

True, M. (2011). *InternQube: Professional skills for the workplace.* Pennsylvania: Intrueition.

CHAPTER 6

Effectively Placing Family Studies Majors at Internship Sites: The ECU-LINCS Match Process

Alan C. Taylor, Elizabeth B. Carroll, Sharon M. Ballard, Eboni J. Baugh, and Bryce L. Jorgensen

Many Family Studies programs offer or require internships for their students (Ballard & Carroll, 2005). The internship is usually the capstone of students' academic preparation and can be pursued in a variety of social, educational, or community-based service agencies (Taylor & Ballard, 2012). An agency or on-site supervisor directs the students' work at the assigned agency or organization. Although the structure (e.g., number of credit hours, number of contact hours) of family science internships varies greatly (Ballard & Carroll, 2005), internships overall are considered a high-impact activity (Kuh, 2008). High-impact practices are deemed

---

A.C. Taylor (✉) • E.B. Carroll • S.M. Ballard
Department of Human Development and Family Science, East Carolina University, Greenville, NC, USA

E.J. Baugh
Department of Human Development and Family Science, Greenville, NC, USA

B.L. Jorgensen
Department of Extension Family and Consumer Sciences, New Mexico State University, Las Cruces, NM, USA

© The Author(s) 2017
T. Newman, A. Schmitt (eds.), *Field-Based Learning in Family Life Education*, DOI 10.1007/978-3-319-39874-7_6

effective because they (1) require that students spend considerable time and effort on purposeful tasks, (2) increase the likelihood that students will come into contact with people who are different than themselves, thereby experiencing diversity, (3) allow students to receive frequent feedback on their performance, mainly from their internship supervisor, (4) provide opportunities to apply learning in a setting that is different than the classroom, and (5) can be a life changing experience in that students gain a greater understanding of themselves in relation to others.

Historically, family science programs have prepared students for positions in higher education or early childhood teaching. Brock (1987) identified the need for more professional training in family science programs that would lead to a new type of helping profession focused on prevention and education. Even though the field has made great strides in skills-based prevention and education training, university faculty are continually searching for ways to better equip students with the necessary knowledge, skills, and experiences to be effective family life educators (Taylor & Ballard, 2012). In order to make this skills and experience emphasis translate into actual practice, many university programs are requiring community-based learning experiences such as internships. Hands-on learning results in professionals who are well-prepared to make a positive impact on families and better equipped to be effective family life educators (Taylor & Ballard, 2012).

Over the past two decades, scholars and educators have advocated for a sequence of pre-professional skill-based experiences for family science students (Keim, 1993; Smart, Keim, Pritchard, & Herron-Miller, 1995). Community agency supervisors have indicated that interns need to be prepared in professional practice prior to the internship (Keim, 1993) and many programs have now incorporated a logical progression of coursework that leads the student to the internship as a capstone experience (Ballard & Carroll, 2005). Additionally, Kuh (2008), in his report on high-impact learning activities for students, suggests that at least one high-impact activity, such as service-learning, be available to students every year.

Consequently, integrating the preparation for internship with the academic program through a proper sequencing of courses and attention to pre-professional practice (Keim, 1993; Smart et al., 1995) may increase the effectiveness of the internship for both students and community partners. Increasingly, community-based service-learning to provide students with "real world" experiences is being incorporated into family studies programs (Ballard & Carroll, 2005; Galbraith, 2002; Ritblatt & Obegi, 2001, Taylor & Ballard, 2012) and frequently is a central component of Certified Family Life Education programs (Taylor & Ballard, 2012). This increase in service-learning along with the careful sequencing of courses is an effective way to meet the need for pre-internship skill building.

6.1 Internships and High-Impact Practices

Providing students with successful internship experiences can directly relate to the *high-impact practices* (Kuh, 2008) students should be exposed to in their academic programs. The internship experience and service-learning component of an undergraduate program allows for *authentic connections to be made with peers, faculty, community, and the university*. These experiences provide students the opportunity to interact with community agency directors and the individuals and families that these agencies serve. The internship is designed to bridge the content and theories learned within the classroom to various community and "real world" experiences. When successfully implemented, the internship *activities and experiences are designed to provide applications to different settings on/off campus* and students are exposed to a variety of community needs and programs that meet those needs. In addition, student interns are often exposed to *diversity through contact with people who are different than themselves,* whether the differences are related to race, gender, socioeconomic status, age, etc.

By providing internship and community experiences for students in our family studies field, faculty, students, and community partners work together to discuss successful ways of securing an internship, expectations while at an internship, and making a real difference in the lives of children, adults and families. This preparation information and interface activities for securing internships provide opportunities in which *faculty and student peers interact about substantive matters.* The issues and ideas discussed will eventually help students secure a job upon graduation and be successful at that job. Using the internship as a job-preparation approach also allows *students to spend considerable amounts of time on the meaningful tasks.* Selecting and securing the right internship and being successful at the internship site are all tasks that will lead to securing and maintaining a job upon graduation.

6.2 The ECU-LINCS Match Process

The internship at East Carolina University (ECU) is a required nine-credit course that students complete in their last semester of the Family and Community Services (FCS) program. Students complete 340 hours at their internship site over the course of one semester. We have an average of 50 interns per semester in the FCS program and only offer internship opportunities during fall and spring semesters. In an effort to bring order to the process of placing students in internships, the Family and Community Services faculty at ECU's Department of Child Development and Family Relations developed the ECU-LINCS (Linking Interns and Community Services) Match Process. The match process is based upon the National Residency Match process for medical students, which was established over 50 years ago to bring order to the process of hospitals recruiting medial residents (Mullin & Stalnaker, 1951). Prior to 1952, medical students were increasingly pressured to make quick decisions regarding their residency (Roth, 2003). F.J. Mullins, the dean of students at the University of Chicago Medical School, proposed a plan whereby students would rank order their choice of residency programs, hospitals would rank order their choice of students, and a match would be produced based on mutual preference (Mullin & Stalnaker, 1951). By design, the match favors the applicant as much as possible (Roth, 2003). The purpose of developing a similar match method for the Family and Community Services program was to design a controlled intern assignment process which was more efficient for students, faculty, and internship sites and increase the likelihood of fit between agency and student. The process is comprised of the following ten steps.

6.2.1 Step One: Internship Orientation

During the semester just prior to a student's internship, students must register for a one-credit-hour Professional Seminar course. This pre-internship course, required for all FCS majors, serves as the internship orientation and is typically taught by the Internship Coordinator. The Internship Coordinator is the same instructor for both the Professional Seminar class and the nine-credit-hour Internship Field Experience Course. The seminar is designed to assist students in securing a field placement location. Further, the seminar instructor contributes to the overall preparation for the internship experience by providing necessary instruction and training to increase the likelihood that students will have a successful internship experience. We believe that a successful experience can ultimately be attributed to a student's attitude, work ethic and pre-internship preparation, so these are points of emphasis in the Professional Seminar.

6.2.2 Step Two: Family and Community Services Internship Fair

Early in the semester, students enrolled in the Professional Seminar attend the Family and Community Services (FCS) Internship Fair. This allows prospective interns to meet students currently involved in their internship. Those students currently interning are required to develop an educational display of their internship site describing the goals and objectives of the agency's services. With 30–45 displays, these posters allow current interns an opportunity to share their experiences with those seeking an internship for the upcoming semester. Community agencies that do not have an FCS intern that particular semester are also encouraged to participate. The prospective interns ask questions that will help determine which agency will provide them with career-building opportunities and learning experiences that meet their career goals. Prospective interns are encouraged to ask presenters questions such as—What does your agency do? What are your specific responsibilities? And knowing what you know now, what would you have done differently in securing your internship?

After the fair, students typically have a better understanding of where they would like to secure an internship. Students should leave the fair having at least three or four placement sites in mind that are consistent with their career aspirations. It is also important that the student is genuinely attracted to the agency's interests. We emphasize that students should not leave the fair without having the necessary contact information for the desired agency.

If students do not find their ideal internship site, our program also provides a comprehensive list of all FCS internship sites available, which includes over 150 agencies. With an extensive list of internship sites, we firmly believe that there is an appropriate internship site for every student. Additionally, we continually add new internship sites that might be consistent with an individual student's interests. Students are then encouraged to do additional investigating with their short lists in order to understand agency objectives and what career benefits an organization specifically offers.

6.2.3 Step Three: Contacting Potential Internship Agencies

After the internship fair and the orientation to the ECU-LINCS Match Process presented during their seminar class, students are instructed to contact their top agency choices. Students are encouraged to call or e-mail the agency's director or use the contact method preferred by the director and to contact them promptly. First impressions, even over the phone or through e-mail are influential, thus students are instructed to maintain a cheerful and professional disposition whenever they are corresponding with agency directors. After initial contact, students and agency directors designate a meeting time at the agency's site, so the director and the potential intern can better determine if the agency is a good fit for the student.

6.2.4   Step Four: Updating the Résumé

Students are instructed to bring an effective résumé when meeting each agency director. Students develop a résumé in the introductory course for the major. One of the early assignments within the seminar is to update previous résumés. FCS faculty collaborate with staff from the career center to teach students how to effectively build and regularly update their résumés in order to emphasize their strengths and assets. Résumés typically include educational background, academic knowledge-base, skill-sets, and out-of-classroom experiences such as the service-learning and volunteer experiences they have accumulated as a university student. An effective résumé should show a potential agency director what knowledge, skills, and abilities students will bring to their agency.

6.2.5   Step Five: Site Visits and Interviews

At appointed times, students meet with the directors at those agencies they have contacted. In addition to bringing a résumé, it is important for the prospective intern to be punctual and to dress appropriately. During the seminar course, students are taught to wear business casual attire to these interviews. It is also emphasized that students should strive for a positive first impression when meeting the director, as it has the potential to build and sustain a good working relationship. While the director will be the primary interviewer, the student, as an interviewee, has been trained to also have some prepared questions to ask, such as:

1. What types of activities are interns asked to do on a regular basis?
2. What are your expectations regarding weekly working hours?
3. In what ways might I gain Family Life Education experience in this internship?

6.2.6   Step Six: ECU-LINCS Rank Form

After interviewing with at least three agencies, the student completes the ECU-LINCS Student Rank Form. This form provides future interns the opportunity to rank each agency based on their preference. In addition to ranking each internship site, the student describes their rationale for each choice. This form is essential to the ECU-LINCS Match Process. Failure to fill out a Student Rank Form results in students being assigned an internship site by the internship coordinator solely based on availability. These rank forms are submitted to the internship coordinator and are typically due on the first week in November for the fall semester or April for the spring semester.

In addition to the Student Ranking Form, each agency director who has interviewed potential interns completes their own ECU-LINCS Agency Rank Form. The internship coordinator corresponds with the agencies to keep them informed of the Match Process and to make sure procedures and deadlines are consistent. The Agency Rank Form is completed by the directors only after the pre-determined interviewing deadline date has passed. The form is typically sent directly to the internship coordinator or is submitted electronically or though the postal mail in advance of the deadline.

Throughout the process, students are reminded that interviews are imperative for securing an internship. Those who fail to interview will not appear on any Agency Rank Form. We also stress that being interviewed at a particular agency does not guarantee placement on that agency's ranking list. Internships are competitive, and sometimes agencies will interview 10–12 potential interns, for 1–2 available internship spots. A potential intern must employ their best interview skills and have an impressive résumé to influence the director's decision to include them on their top five ranking form.

6.2.7   Step Seven: Matchmaking

The internship coordinator, with input as needed from the FCS faculty members, reviews the ranking forms from both the students and the agencies to discern a best fit for the students and the agencies. Typically, most students are placed with either their first or second agency choices.

6.2.8 Step Eight: ECU-LINCS Announcement Gathering

The internship coordinator places the new internship assignments in a letter for each student. This letter designates their upcoming internship site and urges the student to contact the agency immediately. These envelopes are typically handed out at a special gathering. We have tried to make this event a celebration, as the students are anxious and excited to find out where they will be interning. Within our department, we have labeled our gathering as the "LINCS ANNOUNCEMENT PARTY" and have often served refreshments.

6.2.9 Step Nine: Assignment Acceptance

Students contact the agency director within 2–3 days of receiving their internship assignment letter. If the student has any concerns about their assignment, they are encouraged to contact the internship coordinator immediately before accepting the placement. It is important for students to respond in a timely manner because the agency directors are eagerly awaiting their response.

6.2.10 Step Ten: Begin Internship

After going through the LINCS Match Process, students will be ready to begin their internship on the first week of classes the following semester. If required by their university, students generally pay their liability internship insurance before starting at their agency. On the first day, interns are instructed to arrive a few minutes early. Interns are also encouraged to have a positive outlook as they embark on their experience, and to remember that their internship will provide them with valuable learning opportunities towards their future career goals. Finally, interns are reminded to act professionally at their agency as they are representing ECU and the Family and Community Services program.

6.3 Evaluation and Conclusion

Through our preliminary evaluation of the LINCS Match Process, we have found this procedure to be effective in meeting the needs of the students, faculty and agencies/internship supervisors. Our evaluation of the process found that about 75 % of our students are placed in their first choice agency with more than 82 % getting either their first or second choice. Only about 5 % of the students are placed at agencies that represented their fourth or fifth choices. For those who are placed with their fourth or fifth choices, we have found that these students have typically ranked as their top choices certain agencies that only take 1–2 interns. These same internship sites were often highly sought after by 10–15 students each and students were advised of the agencies' competitiveness. We have found that approximately 70 % of internship placements are the first choice of the student and the first choice of the agency. For some of our more outstanding students, it is not uncommon for them to be ranked as the first choice on three or four Agency Rank Forms submitted by the agency directors. This high percentage of first choice matching indicates to us that this process is working well for the great majority of both the students and internship site directors.

At many universities, internship placement processes can be difficult and challenging for students, faculty and the agencies. However, we have found that by developing the ECU-LINCS Match Process it has eased the burden for all involved. Students feel empowered and more informed through this process. The internship fair gives students opportunities to learn more about internship sites and their activities. The fair also allows the prospective interns opportunity to interact with current interns, who are typically excited to share information about the programs and activities in which they are involved. Agency directors feel empowered as well, as they have reported liking the ability to formally interview and rank potential interns. Some agency directors report that they have been able to streamline their own internship selection process by only having to designate one day in which they do their internship interviews. The process also prepares students to successfully apply and secure jobs after they graduate because the ECU-LINCS Match Process simulates the actual hiring process, giving students the opportunity to practice interviewing. ECU-LINCS truly links students, community agencies, and university faculty as they collaborate in the internship placement decision-making.

References

Ballard, S. M., & Carroll, E. B. (2005). Internship practices in family studies programs. *Journal of Family and Consumer Sciences, 97*(4), 11–17.

Brock, G. W. (1987). Family science undergraduate programs: Time for a new approach? *Family Science Review, 1*, 74–78.

Galbraith, K. A. (2002). Integrating service learning into human service and family science curriculum. *Journal of Teaching and Marriage and Family, 2*(4), 363–384.

Keim, R. E. (1993). Professional practices in family science: Essential for an undergraduate course. *Family Science Review, 6*(1, 2), 73–79.

Kuh, G. D. (2008). *High-impact educational practices: What they are, who has access to them, and why they matter.* Washington, DC: Association of American Colleges and Universities.

Mullin, F. J., & Stalnaker, J. M. (1951). The matching plan of internship appointment. *Journal of Medical Education, 26,* 341–345.

Ritblatt, S. N., & Obegi, A. D. (2001). Community-based service-learning in family sciences: Course development and learning outcomes. *Journal of Teaching and Marriage and Family, 1,* 45–64.

Roth, A. E. (2003). The origins, history, and design of the resident match. *Journal of the American Medical Association., 289*(7), 909–912.

Smart, L. S., Keim, R. E., Pritchard, M. E., & Herron-Miller, A. C. (1995). Professional development during college: A comparison of out-of-class experiences in two majors. *Family Science Review, 8*(3, 4), 129–141.

Taylor, A. C., & Ballard, S. M. (2012). Preparing students to work with diverse populations. In S. M. Ballard & A. C. Taylor (Eds.), *Family life education with diverse populations* (pp. 285–302). Thousand Oaks, CA: Sage Publications Inc.

CHAPTER 7

Developing Connections: Using an On-Campus Event to Connect HDFS Students and the Community

Laura Landry-Meyer and Michael R. Sturm Jr.

Developing Connections is an on-campus event that extends the classroom connecting students to the real world through community agencies. The event creates and maintains strong community partnerships and alumni relations while simultaneously being a valuable recruitment and retention tool. Human Development and Family Studies (HDFS) undergraduate students, community professionals, alumni, and the university community connect through direct interaction during formal interviews or informal poster displays.

For students, Developing Connections encourages exploration of the many career possibilities afforded by a broad family science education. The curriculum at our university has received program approval from the National Council of Family Relations following the Family Life Education (FLE) framework. The ten FLE content areas (see ncfr.org) are utilized across a life span perspective. Developing Connections provides a "real-

---

L. Landry-Meyer (✉)
Human Development and Family Studies, Bowling Green State University, Bowling Green, OH, USA

M.R. Sturm Jr.
Human Development and Family Studies, Penn State Brandywine, Media, PA, USA

© The Author(s) 2017
T. Newman, A. Schmitt (eds.), *Field-Based Learning in Family Life Education*, DOI 10.1007/978-3-319-39874-7_7

life" experience for students as a means to "see" life stage and FLE content areas in action. Students are exposed to new internship and career paths that they may not have considered or knew existed before attending the event.

Specific high-impact practice and engagement principles are embedded in the HDFS curriculum and implemented at Developing Connections. Introduced by Alexander Astin (1984), student engagement is conceptualized as the time and effort students devote to activities. Kuh (2008, 2009) identified interaction with faculty, interaction with peers, and in-class/academic engagement as engagement factors. Chickering and Gamson's (1987) principles of good practice in undergraduate education promote student engagement focusing on student/faculty contact, cooperation among students, active learning, prompt feedback, time on task, communication of high expectations, and the respect for diversity. These student engagement principles support the high-impact practices outlined by the American Association of Colleges and Universities (2007). A synthesis of student engagement and high-impact practices will be used to describe Developing Connections as an embedded field-based learning event.

7.1 Developing Connections: An On-Campus Event

Developing Connections engages students with exposure to professionals in the community. It is a unique field-based learning experience being held on campus as a means to facilitate engagement in community. Field experiences are considered systematic opportunities to observe and assist a current professional in a community-based setting where students can "practice" their skills (Capraro, Capraro, & Helfeldt, 2010).

Developing Connections is structured as a poster display, professional development, and networking event held each spring and fall semester prior to midterms. Students network with professionals, faculty, alumni, and each other in an interactive environment through professional development roundtables, a keynote speaker, intern, and organization poster presentations and on-site internship interviews. The specific event objectives are to facilitate potential internship placements between organizations and students, enhance collaboration among child and family community organizations, assist students in exploring potential careers, and provide a forum for on-site interviews.

Student engagement in the Developing Connections varies based on course enrollment at the introductory, pre-internship, and internship level. These three levels go beyond the recommendation that students participate in at least two high-impact practices in their first year and senior year (Kuh, 2008; National Survey of Student Engagement [NSSE], 2007). These levels are embedded within the HDFS curriculum—each level has specific assessment and student reflections that are coordinated based on course enrollment. Brownell and Swaner (2009) report that designing field-based experiences carefully with a focus on specific campus and curriculum goals increases the likelihood of strong educational outcomes which we feel has occurred through Developing Connections.

At the introductory level, Developing Connections is integrated into a pre-professional, seminar course introducing students to the family science profession. As a first-year experience, the course provides a forum for students to investigate and potentially secure a job-shadowing experience.

At the pre-internship level, Developing Connections is integrated into a course designed to lead students through a process of self-assessment, prioritization of career preferences, and the acquisition of professional development skills and ethics in an internship/employment setting. Students are encouraged to utilize the FLE framework and develop a personalized sound bite to explain their preferred life stage and content area. Knowing oneself and learning to articulate that professional identity is key. Students learn strategies to present themselves in a professional manner to potential internship sites and employers.

At the internship level, current interns create and present a poster about their internship placement site which is a type of capstone project (Kuh, 2008). The poster displays their site's mission, services offered, location(s), contact information, and specific duties or activities performed by an intern. Interns present their poster to their peers, faculty, alumni, and professionals highlighting experiences. Interns have opportunities to share insight with other students who are interested in HDFS, are just starting out in the major, or about to embark on their internship experience.

7.2 High-Impact Practice Elements

Based on a synthesis of student engagement and high-impact practices, four elements will be used to describe Developing Connections as an embedded field-based learning event: time on meaningful tasks, interaction on substantive matters, activities applicable on/off campus, and authentic connections.

7.2.1 Students Spend Considerable Amounts of Time on Meaningful Tasks

Embedded learning activities demand student investment of time to purposeful tasks associated with professional development. Early in their undergraduate career, students are integrated into Developing Connections as means for increasing their understanding of future career options. Attendance at Developing Connections deepens the commitment to investing time in courses as students can "see" the path to internship and graduation making coursework relevant. Students tend to spend considerable amounts of time on relevant self-assessments that contribute to career development. Career-related assignments project a student's professional identity and meet the developmental need of career identification (Landry-Meyer & Roe, 2013). Students who perceived their coursework and field experience (internship) to be relevant self-rate their competence in the field setting higher (Capraro et al., 2010). Congruent coursework with field-based work is effective when perceived as relevant and meaningful.

7.2.2 Faculty and Student Peers Interact About Substantive Matters

Kuh (2008, 2009) reports that students who talk about substantive matters are challenged to perform at higher levels. Articulating who you are as a professional requires an integration of developmental tasks of identity, career, fidelity to values, lifestyle—an integration of a person's worldview. Students' expression of their career interests provides a framework for them to articulate a professional identity and show their knowledge of theory and research in their chosen area. The career objective projects one's values based on career choice respecting each student's worldview and career aims (Landry-Meyer & Roe, 2013).

7.2.3 Activities Have Applications to Different Settings On/Off Campus

The multifaceted aspect of the Developing Connections event means student activities are not merely a one-time instance but rather a primer for future professional activities and the real world. Since the event is held each fall and spring semester, undergraduate HDFS students have multiple exposure to this high-impact event and thus many opportunities to develop in the areas of networking, presentation, and interviewing over the course of their college career. As students' progress through the major, their level of participation grows ensuring they have developed both the skill and confidence to move toward more challenging levels of participation such as interviewing for an internship placement or presenting their internship experience. Students' repeated exposure to this high-impact event has the potential to positively impact their engagement in undergraduate education (Kuh, 2007).

In the future, it is expected that students will be required to interview for employment or graduate school admissions, deliver professional presentations, attend professional development offerings, and network throughout their career. The overarching thread among these activities relates to competency in one's interpersonal skills. Interpersonal skills are fundamental to employability and even more so to employability in the family field where such skills are required to educate and deliver services in a professional capacity. With the increase in technology-driven classrooms and online courses and in an age where students are communicating via technology at increasing rates, opportunities for students to develop interpersonal skills have potentially diminished. The Developing Connections event provides a compressed opportunity for students to develop and apply such skills. For example, mock graduate school interviews are provided for more senior students as a means for developing their knowledge and comfort in the graduate school interview process while simultaneously receiving feedback on their presentation and responses. In addition to its programmatic goals, Developing Connections can build a student's skill level for seeking on-campus employment or securing a volunteer opportunity while completing their studies.

7.2.4 Authentic Connections Are Made with Peers, Faculty, Community, and University

Interns are able to connect with first-year and pre-internship students through poster presentations at Developing Connections. Interacting with those "new-to-the-major" and peers allows interns to demonstrate what it takes to succeed in the major and obtain a relevant internship. Kuh (2007) notes that while this interaction of demonstrating to newcomers is necessary, it must also be supported by other connections to faculty and university resources.

Faculty value and participate in Developing Connections often serving as on-site interviewers, roundtable discussants, or day-off mentors interacting informally with students. When faculty value a high-impact event like Developing Connections, students are more likely to participate and benefit (Kuh, 2008). The college has acknowledged the value and has endorsed the event with support in the planning and implementation. Kuh (2008) notes when the university endorses the worth of an activity, the campus culture is likely to encourage student participation. The vast majority of HDFS majors attend Developing Connections at least three times during their undergraduate career.

Authentic connections are made and maintained with professionals during the event. The presence of an external audience (alumni, professionals) creates a realistic expectation about career preparation. Many professionals are alumni who are genuine in their mentorship and advice and recruitment of interns.

7.3 Implementation

The implementation of a Developing Connections-type event requires collaboration between local community agencies, faculty, and the university. A faculty member needs to be identified as the point of contact for the event and the relationships between all stakeholders. Although several faculty members can participate in planning, it is best that stakeholders have only one person to communicate with regarding event logistics. The event is best suited for an academic program which requires an internship component. The internship component serves as the backbone of the event and the foundation for event activities.

7.3.1 Community Partnerships

Developing Connections relies on partnerships between local community organizations and the university. Many human service organizations and non-profits rely on personnel such as interns to sustain the services they provide. Alliances can be built with local community organizations by assessing their mission and scope in relation to your academic program.

- Does the mission of the organization highlight aspects of the academic program?
- Would a graduate from the program be eligible to work for this organization?
- Would a student in the program gain valuable workplace experience as a member of this organization?
- Is the organization open to hosting an intern in exchange for mentorship experience and guidance?

This assessment is the first step in determining if local community organizations have a need and can support a student intern.

7.3.2 Faculty Support

Program faculty must buy-in to the event for it to be successful. Their ability to see the event as important and valuable for students will reflect in student engagement (National Survey of Student Engagement [NSSE], 2007). Collectively faculty members can ensure the event successful and a high-impact experience for students by:

- Requiring students to participate in the event.
- Volunteering at the event to support the event and develop relationships with students in the major.
- Developing meaningful assignments to assist students participating in the event.
- Cultivating relationships with students and community agencies at the event.

Faculty support is imperative to execute the event and garner support from the larger university.

7.3.3 University Support

Although not required, support from the university makes a larger statement to event participants regarding the event's importance and the university's willingness to partner with the community. University support can come in the means of:

- funding;
- space provisions;
- administrative support; and
- programmatic contributions.

For example, at past Developing Connections events, the college has provided refreshments and other campus offices such as the Office of Graduate Studies and Career Services have lent their expertise by sending representatives to orchestrate professional development roundtables.

7.3.4 Programmatic Alignment

When planning the event, the academic program should be considered. The event best meets the needs of students if it is embedded in several areas of the program: introductory, pre-internship, and internship. Faculty should determine which courses best fit with each level of students' progression through the program. This enables the event to become an experience embedded in particular courses. Once this is determined, faculty of the embedded courses can then work to develop meaningful tasks for students to complete.

7.3.5 Students

Students must be prepared for the event and aware of its valuable nature. For pre-interns, the culmination of career objective/sound bite, résumé, and interview skills occurs at Developing Connections. These students are required to participate in at least one on-site interview to practice their statements to an external audience. The on-site interviews are a win-win situation for students and agencies. Agencies have the opportunity to recruit interns and entry-level employees. Students have the opportunity to practice their skills and find an internship. Students respond positively to the interviews—they report feeling more confident after having completed an interview. In addition, they gain experience networking with professionals, develop professional résumés in preparation for interviews, and have an opportunity to self-reflect on their interviewing skills and personal fit with agencies based on course assignments.

7.3.6 Event Planning

When implementing an event like Developing Connections, the size and scope of the event can vary. An initial event can start small and build throughout subsequent semesters based on feedback and need. The first step in event planning is determining what you hope to offer and balancing this with feasibility and the resources at hand. Some possible event activities include:

- on-site internship interviews;
- a human services poster fair;
- professional development roundtables;
- a networking time with refreshments or meal; and
- an alumni panel.

Once the scope of the event has been determined, contact should be made with potential participants including faculty, students, alumni, community agencies, and other university personnel. This contact should highlight the proposed agenda for the event and allow attendees to determine their level of participation. Participation will dictate space needs as well as the following:

- tables, chairs, podium;
- signage;
- refreshments;
- university personnel; and
- faculty assistance with the event.

After knowing who intends to participate, a final agenda can be developed.

7.3.7 Feedback and Assessment

Prior to the event, plan to solicit participant feedback. Have attendees reflect on aspects of the event and use their suggestions to build upon what you have developed. For each event, on-site evaluation forms are given to agencies in attendance and the point of contact circulates during the event soliciting informal feedback. Developing Connections has evolved based on feedback from agencies resulting in a more structured on-site interview process.

Student feedback is obtained through reflection assignments from introductory students and seminar discussions with pre-internship and intern students. Student feedback has contributed to the addition of a keynote speaker and opening session followed by roundtables focusing on specific professional development skills.

7.4   FINAL THOUGHTS

Each relationship, whether it is with a community agency or college administrator, takes time to build. The "relationship building" aspect of the event is a long-standing task throughout the year. It should be noted that the current Developing Connections event was initiated in 2005 and has grown and changed since its inception. Growth and change to the event reflects current student needs as well as more deeply forged connections developed with agencies, alumni, and university personnel.

REFERENCES

Association of American Colleges and Universities, The National Leadership Council for Liberal Education and America's Promise. (2007). *College Learning for the New Global Century*. Retrieved from http://www.aacu.org/leap/documents/GlobalCentury_final.pdf

Astin, A. (1984). Student involvement: A developmental theory for higher education. *Journal of College Student Personnel, 25*(4), 297–308.

Brownell, J. E., & Swaner, L. E. (2009). High impact practices: Applying the learning outcomes literature to the development of successful campus programs. *Peer Review*, 26–30. *Also appeared in Diversity & Democracy: http://www.diversityweb.org/DiversityDemocracy/vol12no2/brownell.cfm

Capraro, M. M., Capraro, R. M., & Helfeldt, J. (2010). Do differing types of field experiences make a difference in teacher candidates' perceived level of competence? *Teacher Education Quarterly, 37*, 131–154.

Chickering, A. W., & Gamson, Z. F. (1987). Seven principles for good practice in undergraduate education. *AAHE Bulletin, March*, 3–7.

Kuh, G. (2007). What student engagement data tell us about college readiness? *Peer Review, 9*, 4–8 Retrieved from https://www.aacu.org/peerreview/pr-wi07/pr-wi07_analysis1.cfm.

Kuh, G. (2008). *High-impact educational practices: What they are, who has access to them, and why they matter.* Washington, DC: AAC&U.

Kuh, G. (2009). What student affairs professionals need to know about student engagement. *Journal of College Student Personnel, 50*, 683–706.

Landry-Meyer, L., & Roe, J. R. (2013). Linking teaching methods and assessment to the developmental needs of family science students. *Family Science Review, 18*(1), 117–133.

National Survey of Student Engagement (NSSE). (2007). *Experiences that matter: Enhancing student learning and success.* Bloomington: Indiana University Center for Postsecondary Research.

CHAPTER 8

Learning to Observe and Interpret Behavior as a High-Impact Practice Within Family Science Courses

Dave Riley

As a practice-based field of study, we teach not only knowledge but also skills. In this, we have something in common with fields such as nursing and architecture. Because skilled behaviors can only be learned through actual practice, usually with feedback from an expert, all these fields of study emphasize practice-based learning in the real world. They emphasize "learning by doing" with high-impact experiences.

Among the skills that are most foundational in family life education, and indeed across all the human service fields, is the ability to observe and interpret behavior. Fifty years ago, a course with that idea in its title, "Observing and Interpreting Child Behavior," was commonly offered in programs of child and family study. Today, this course has largely disappeared, but the skill it taught is no less important for those who intend to work in parenting education, couples counseling, early childhood education, or other family life fields.

D. Riley (✉)
Human Ecology, University of Wisconsin–Madison, Madison, WI, USA

8.1 The Use of Observation in Two Courses

I teach the skill of observing and interpreting behavior through two courses, one on Parenting Education and the other on Child Development. In each course, students have off-campus placements for the semester where they can make direct observations of child or parent-child behaviors. Weekly assignments to write observations help the students learn to apply the course concepts to extract greater meaning from what they observe. That is the primary aim of the observation assignments: to learn to see the world through the course constructs, and thereby to see it with greater meaning, and to really understand the concepts. A second purpose is to learn to write in a way that clearly and consistently separates our objective observations from our subjective interpretations (a skill that, for example, physicians, nurses, social workers, therapists, and others must master). Lastly, students produce a professional product, usually a newsletter for their placement site, at the end of the semester.

The basic assignment is simple. Write an observation that illustrates one or more concepts from the course, breaking the written report into two parts with these subheads: "What we saw," and "What it means." The first part, the observation, should be objective, descriptive, and clear. It should use exact quotes if people spoke, and provide details and descriptive language to communicate unobservable factors such as emotional states ("Her eyes opened wide" rather than "she was surprised"). A great observation tells a small story.

The second part of the written report is the interpretation. I ask students to use one or more concepts from the course to interpret and add meaning to the observation. They should highlight and unobtrusively define the concepts they use, and refer back to the specifics of the observation to justify each concept. A really good interpretation will provide a larger context and significance to the observation by explaining why this particular part of parenting or child development is important (e.g., how it predicts later outcomes). The sample observations below show how succinctly this can be done. And writing succinctly is our aim.

In some classes, I have the students bring to class 3 copies of their one-page observation report, and in groups of three they critique each other's writing. Students then revise their observations before turning them in.

The in-class writing lab is especially useful for the weaker writers in the class, as they see firsthand what the excellent writing of other students' looks like, and they understand why it is good writing by having to critique it. Each week, I also show 2–3 observation reports that have noteworthy strengths (making sure to share one from every student over the course of the term), projecting them on the overhead screen for discussion. Besides discussing the exemplary aspects of each, we also play the game of guessing what meaning the writer extracted from their observation. For example, read the first paragraph of the sample observation from one of my students shown below. Cover the second paragraph ("What it means") with your hand. Try guessing what meaning you might extract from this observation and then lift your hand to see what the writer did with it. Doing this as a class consistently led to unexpected insights and meanings that I had not anticipated. It also led to two consistent insights: (1) observing takes active effort, the opposite of passive activities like watching TV or listening to music; and (2) even very simple and short observations can generate great amounts of meaning to a person who is prepared with the concepts of our field.

8.2 Student Observation 1 (Parenting)

8.2.1 What We Saw

While a mother and her four-year-old waited in the check-out line at the market, her son looked over the vast candy selection. He touched none, but asked his mother three different times, "Can I get one of these?" pointing to different candies each time. As the mother loaded her groceries onto the conveyor belt, she first responded by saying "no" without turning or looking at her son. The second time, she raised her voice saying, "Boy, I already told you no. You aren't getting no candy tonight." With his third request, the mother stopped, turned to face her son, lowered her voice and said, "How many times do I have to tell you?" The mother then grabbed her son by the forearm and pulled him away from the candy to the bagging area. The son stood still, looking down until the mother was finished paying. The mother then pushed the cart forward and the son walked behind her, following the mother out of the store.

8.2.2 What It Means

The *Can Do* skill is a parenting technique that equips parents and caregivers to redirect unacceptable behavior, by following four steps: notice what you don't want your child to do, think of something else your child can do instead, tell your child what they can do, and help your child if it is necessary. The *Can Do* skill allows parents to establish limits and boundaries, while teaching competent behavior.

The mother above could have readily employed the *Can Do* skill, reducing her frustration and her son's. For example, she could have said "We're not getting candy today, but you can help me by placing our items on the conveyor belt." Although he was too small to reach to the bottom of the cart, she could have handed him items to place on the conveyor belt (step 4 of the skill: help your child if needed). This would have been a *Teaching Do* statement, in which she was teaching her son how to do the activity (shopping) competently. Overall, the *Can Do* skill helps parents teach competent behaviors that can replace behaviors they find unacceptable, which can lead to less conflict, warmer parent-child relations, and a more competent child.

8.3 Student Observation 2 (Child Development)

8.3.1 What We Saw

During music time, three children including three-year-old Charlie immediately ran over to the only piano in the classroom. The teacher then explained to the three children, "We have to take turns, because everyone wants to have a turn at the piano. Let's wait patiently so all our friends can have a turn." Charlie immediately began looking around and then picked up a small maraca. With the maraca in his hand, he walked over to a mat and laid down. He shook the maraca a few times, looked over at the piano and then looked back at the maraca. After doing this several times, he started humming to himself while shaking the maraca.

8.3.2 What It Means

During music time, Charlie was able to avoid frustration by *substituting a new goal* for himself with the maraca instead of the piano. *Substituting a new goal* means that a child is able to pick another activity that they enjoy in place of the first and be comfortable with doing that activity instead. By using this *impulse control* technique, Charlie was able to focus his attention on the maraca and distract himself from the piano. At one point, he even hummed to himself and moved further away to regulate his emotions more easily. The ability of children to self-regulate emotions is an early predictor of their ability to calm themselves without acting out (*frustration tolerance*), to be less impulsive in years to come, and to do better in their future schooling.

Student Observation #1 is exemplary in several ways. It used a course concept with precision, defining it and even listing the four steps we use in teaching it. It linked the concept to the specifics of the observation and provided its own example of how the parent might have used the parenting skill. In the final sentence, it also explained the developmental significance of the concept. Finally, the writing was admirably succinct, with no unnecessary words. The second student observation is even more succinct (the student cut its length almost in half while revising the first draft).

At the end of the semester, each student packages several of their observations into a newsletter for the programs at which they observed, written in an informative and entertaining style that the program can distribute to its participants. The programs really appreciate these, and do actually copy and distribute them. The students understand that they have produced something of value, which they could use as a work sample when applying for jobs.

8.4 Featured High-Impact Learning Experiences

Several features of this instructional method align with the definition of high-impact learning experiences provided by a publication of the American Association of Colleges and Universities (Kuh, 2008), in particular the following:

8.4.1 Students Spend Considerable Amounts of Time on Meaningful Tasks

The students are placed in real-world worksites to do their observations. We even discuss how to present oneself professionally, as representatives of the university. The students are sometimes surprised to realize that the professional staff wants to see their written observations and find value in them. It becomes clear to the students that this task is more than just a class assignment, but has actual value in the family services workplace, where the ability of staff to interpret behavior is a key skill.

8.4.2 Students Receive Frequent Performance Feedback

The in-class writing critique circles give students a real experience of learning from each other, and also of learning how to provide a constructive critique of others' work. In this way, they receive feedback from both their peers and from the instructor every week. The students also rate each other on the usefulness of the critiques they receive. Because these peer ratings contribute to the course grades, they become an incentive to very thoughtful feedback sessions.

8.4.3 Faculty and Student Peers Interact About Substantive Matters

For students who have studied the course concepts before, the biggest surprise is usually how much better they understand those concepts after being forced to see them in operation in the real world. Their whole field of study, family science, comes alive in front of them, as they learn to really apply the cognitive schemas of their college learning to their everyday perceptions.

8.4.4 Students Experience Diversity Through Contact with People Who Are Different from Themselves

The community placements often put the students in continuing, semester-long contact with people who are different from themselves and their normal social world, in terms of economic class and ethnicity. This serves one of the goals of our undergraduate program.

8.4.5 Activities Have Applications to Different Settings On/Off Campus

The students aiming to become parent educators or preschool teachers see clearly that they are learning basic skills for their professions, but so do students headed in other directions, such as social work, clinical psychology, education, or occupational therapy. One student who had just been admitted to medical school realized, with surprise that the skill he was learning was exactly what a good physician must master in order to write a diagnosis: what you can objectively observe, and what you can diagnose from it, with a clear boundary between the two.

At the end of the term, each student packages a selection of their written observations into a newsletter for the community program, suitable for the program to use with its clients. The programs value these as solid professional products and actually use them. This demonstration of respect for their work often contributes to students transitioning in their self-concepts, from the self-concept of a student to that of a professional. That is the kind of high impact we seek, as a well-earned side effect of learning professional skills.

Conclusion

This educational practice, teaching students how to observe and interpret behavior by applying concepts from their college course, can be used as part of most family science courses. All that is required is suitable locations to observe the phenomena being studied, whether it is a course in "Adult Development and Aging" or "Family Relationships." Two main aims are accomplished by this form of field-based learning. First, observing and interpreting behavior is a foundational skill for almost any kind of work with families. Indeed, it is a way to turn the knowledge of our courses into the skilled practice of using that knowledge.

Second, learning to observe and interpret behavior brings to life the concepts we are teaching. In family science courses, we do not always have demonstrations available for our constructs, in the way a chemistry or physics course does, through their labs. But an assignment to go out and "capture" the phenomenon under study, through direct observation, provides just this concrete demonstration of our family science concepts.

For the instructor, one of the best parts of using observation as a learning experience is the excitement of the students, many of whom are astonished and thrilled to begin seeing the concepts they have been learning all around them. As if unveiled, their everyday worlds suddenly carry so much more meaning. In the words of the Italian proverb, "To him (or her) that watches, everything is revealed."

Reference

Kuh, G. D. (2008). *High-impact educational practices: What they are, who has access to them, and why they matter.* Washington, DC: Association of American Colleges and Universities.

CHAPTER 9

Learning Through Engagement: A Praxis Approach to Teaching Family Life Education Methodology

Nathan R. Cottle, Jeremy Boden, and Grant Richards

Faculty at universities across the country are putting a pronounced emphasis on more active, hands-on types of learning in an effort to improve education. Although it has many different names (e.g., Engaged Learning, transformative learning, service learning, etc.), the key components of this type of learning are that it is an active, student-led, field-based learning by doing (e.g., Sweet & Michaelsen, 2012; Vazin & Reile, 2006).

This move to more effective types of learning is accomplished through the use of more high-impact practices (HIP; referred to by the associated number below throughout the paper) in the approach to teaching Family Life Education (FLE) methodology:

1. Students spend considerable amounts of time on meaningful tasks.
2. Faculty and student peers interact about substantive matters.
3. Students experience diversity through contact with people who are different than themselves.

N.R. Cottle (✉) • J. Boden
Family Studies, Utah Valley University, Orem, UT, USA

G. Richards
Behavioral Sciences, Utah Valley University, Orem, UT, USA

4. Students receive frequent performance feedback.
5. Activities have applications to different settings on/off campus.
6. Authentic connections are made with peers, faculty, community, and/or the university (Kuh, 2008).

Utah Valley University (UVU) embraced this approach to learning through the Engaged Learning effort, suggesting students could graduate with not only a diploma but a résumé as well. Engaged Learning is the combination of traditional academic and hands-on education. UVU went as far as to create a Center for Engaged Learning which provides faculty and students with Grants for Engaged Learning opportunities, and the Carnegie Foundation classified UVU as a "community engaged" institution.

9.1 UVU Family Studies Emphasis

The Family Studies Emphasis at UVU modified the process of teaching of FLE methodology to match these more active learning approaches and to include more high-impact practices. The change occurred in three separate ways:

1. *The Class*—using meaningful, student-led assignments (HIP 1, 2, and 4) in the methodology course.
2. *The Certification*—certifying students in a widely used family curriculum (HIP 1, 2, 4, and 6).
3. *The Experience*—participating in the Strengthening Families Program (SFP) by teaching diverse families in a field-based setting of campus (HIP 3, 4, 5, and 6).

9.1.1 The Class

The FAMS 4500 FLE methods course is devoted to engaging students in the development, facilitation, and evaluation of a novel family life education curriculum (HIP 1). At first, students are often overwhelmed by the scope of this assignment; however, their fears are often assuaged as they see that smaller tasks are the building blocks to the larger assignment (Duncan & Goddard, 2011; Powell & Cassidy, 2007). Before students begin their assignment, however, they learn the importance of ethics in FLE. Consistent with the statutes of National Council on Family Relations (NCFR), a foundational component to the FAMS 4500 course includes the Family Life Educators Code of Ethics (Adams, Dollahite, Gilbert, & Keim, 1998).

Because collaborative learning can be beneficial to students as they grapple together over strategies, concepts, and learning to work in a group setting (Vazin & Reile, 2006), students form self-selected curriculum teams which usually consist of 3–4 students based on their interest in the topic (Sweet & Michaelsen, 2012). Then, teams are required to draft a *Program Proposal and Problem Statement* explaining why their chosen topic is important to individuals or families. Next, teams conduct a *Needs Assessment*. Team members collaborate to devise questions to glean the *felt needs* of the target population (Arcus, 1993); the assessment is given to at least ten individuals in the target audience. Further, students are required to interview at least one expert in their chosen topic to derive their populations' *ascribed needs* (Arcus, 1993).

Based on their findings from the *Needs Assessment*, teams complete a *Literature Review* (Duncan & Goddard, 2011; Powell & Cassidy, 2007). Students submit a rough draft that is reviewed by the instructor, and given feedback (HIP 1). Teams are then asked to make the suggested changes and resubmit a second draft thereafter.

Once these important pieces are completed, teams are then asked to propose at least four sessions in their curriculum and to begin developing an *Instructor's Guide* for their individual sessions. Each individual is required to develop one 90-minute session as part of their group's curriculum. Teams are also required to develop a *Marketing Plan* which includes how they are going to advertise to their target audience, including the creation of advertisements.

Understandably, the development and presentation of a program can be daunting for many students who often do not have any experience teaching large groups. Therefore, one of the primary goals of the course is to immerse and train students in the art of effective presenting and teaching skills (Duncan & Goddard, 2011). To facilitate this process, four teaching assignments are distributed throughout the semester to allow high levels of faculty-student interaction (HIP 2) and to create a safe environment for performance feedback (HIP 4).

The first teaching assignment requires students to teach for 7–10 minutes on any subject of their choosing. This introductory teaching assignment provides a gentle and safe exposure to standing up in front of a large group. Next, teams present a small portion of an established curriculum for 15–20 minutes. This presentation allows students to not only gain experience with a detailed instructors guide, engaging an audience, and following a pre-designed established program, but also exposes them to teaching as a group.

Next, teams teach the first 30–40 minutes of their *own* program in class (HIP 2). This will also be the first time that the instructor *and* their peers give detailed and specific feedback to the teams presenting (HIP 4). Finally, teams are required to present one entire 90-minute session from their program in front of their peers as well as the instructor. After they present, teams are again given both verbal and written feedback (HIP 2, 4). Students often report that they are able to see their teaching abilities improve over the semester, and they learn the strengths of their design. This feedback allows them to fix any problem areas in their teaching or curriculum.

Finally, teams are required to teach one session of their curriculum to a live audience in a public setting (HIP 1, 3, 4, and 5). This part of the assigned project allows students to experience contact with a more diverse population who may be different than themselves. Students are allowed to teach their program wherever they would like. Audience members are recruited via on-campus signs, advertisement, and student social media. Finally, students are asked to complete a formative evaluation that is based on their own observations as well as the evaluations provided by the program participants.

9.1.2   *The Certification*

In addition to this curriculum assignment, our FAMS 4500 class includes certification training in the *Survival Skills of Healthy Families* curriculum (Family Wellness Associates, 2004). Many past students reported that they needed to already have content to teach their clients before they were hired. They complained they could recite the theorists or identify important terms, but struggle with what to say when a parent asks how to get their child to go to bed. As a result, we began certifying our students in this curriculum to provide them some content to share with their clients and to teach them how to deliver FLE in a group setting.

One member of the faculty is a master trainer for the curriculum and conducts the certification as part of the FAMS 4500 class. Students are certified for three years and are also authorized to use the addition-related curricula focused on premarital and marital couples, stepfamilies, fathers, and families who have experienced domestic violence. The certification experience adds greatly to the methodology class because students learn important FLE techniques, have opportunities to practice and receive feedback as they teach back the material, and learn effective content to share with future clients (HIP 1, 2, and 4). Students learn how to role-play, conduct group activities, sculpt important family dynamics and concepts, and coach individuals to use the skills with their family members. These valuable techniques can be used in a group FLE setting or with an individual client to teach skills. We have begun collecting data to investigate the effectiveness of the inclusion of this certification in the FLE methodology course.

Although not every university has faculty who may be a master trainer of a similar curriculum, university programs should seek out opportunities for additional training for the benefit of their students. Many community agencies or non-profits provide certification opportunities to their employees as part of their mission. Curriculum authors should also be open to allowing their programs to be taught to students as part of their education and preparation to work with individuals and families.

The certification as part of the class places the focus on meaningful tasks of learning and practicing important techniques in teaching (HIP 1). Faculty and students interact back and forth with students learning by seeing and then doing (HIP 2). Students teach the material back to the class in pairs, receiving feedback from other students and faculty, and are given multiple attempts to incrementally improve their craft (HIP 4). Finally, authentic connections are made between peers and faculty as they learn to teach more effectively and gain the confidence needed to present material to the community (HIP 6).

9.1.3 The Experience: Strengthening Families Program

To provide students more field-based opportunities for family life education through rewarding internship experiences (Arcus, 1993), we have focused on truancy and at-risk families in the local school district to deliver FLE. Working with representatives from Alpine School District, Parent Teacher Association (PTA), Juvenile Court, the Division of Child and Family Services (DCFS), Wasatch Mental Health, Orem City, and Latinos In Action (LIA), we created the Strengthening Families Program (SFP), using an evidence-based curriculum (Kumpfer & DeMarsh, 1983). Because we feel this experience offers student-led, hands-on learning, each student in the UVU Family Studies emphasis is trained in this curriculum and teaches in the SFP as part of their degree requirements for at least one semester. Many students repeat the experience for credit or as a volunteer after completing the requirement.

Invitations to attend the SFP go to families recommended by a school's Student Success Team and families that express interest at UVU presentations at Back to School and Parent/Teacher nights. A maximum of 12 families are invited to each program site. Programs meet once a week for 11 weeks at a school within the high school cluster. The program begins with a family dinner at 5:30 p.m. (with food provided by a local church food bank). Then, participants divide into parent, teen, and child classes taught by UVU student interns from 6:00 to 7:00 p.m. Finally, families reunite in a family class from 7:00 to 8:00 p.m., which is also taught exclusively by students. PTA volunteers assist with the preparation of dinner, and LIA members assist with serving, cleanup, and a nursery for the young children. Often classes are offered in Spanish for those parents who do not speak English. Native-speaking students and others who may have served two-year mission trips to Spanish-speaking areas teach these classes. Finally, site supervisors and students gather after the families have left to debrief, discuss any issues, and provide feedback to one another.

The usual budgeted cost of each SFP program is about $14,000. UVU has been able to conduct SFP for Alpine District Schools at no cost to the district or families due to donations and grants, the volunteer labor of faculty, UVU student interns and volunteers, and volunteer assistance from Alpine District personnel, School PTAs, and LIA members. During 2013, UVU provided over 40 interns, and 50 community volunteers participated. During 2013, approximately 50 families were served by the SPF program. These SFP programs have also received Engaged Learning Grants from UVU, food donations from the Church of Jesus Christ of Latter-day Saints, grants from DCFS, and fund-raising by UVU's Family Studies Club. Beginning fall 2013, Brigham Young University has allocated three Master of Social Work (MSW) interns, and UVU has allocated one Bachelor of Social Work (BSW) intern to support SFP and offer counseling and case management support.

The SFP provides students the type of learning and high-impact practices discussed in this work. Specifically, students are engaged in meaningful tasks and experience diversity as they work with families who may have great challenges, including poverty and truancy (HIP 1 and 3). Students teach the classes in an off-campus setting—just as they would in their first job (HIP 5). Each week, students and faculty review the evening's events for opportunities to improve and vicarious learning through the sharing of experiences (HIP 2 and 4). Finally, authentic connections are made between students, faculty, and community members (HIP 6). Students in the SFP often form meaningful relationships with their clients and truly see the change in their lives within the program. This internship experience is the culmination of the learning students have done in class, of the knowledge gained through the certification, and of the experience facilitating the program.

9.2 Conclusion

Our approach to teaching students FLE methodology has changed to be more hands-on and student-led in an effort to improve their learning and abilities. Simply, we teach them to teach, practice having them teach, and then trust them to teach those who need so much of their help. Few other university programs or internship opportunities place so much responsibility in the hands of the students. This approach to teaching FLE methodology matches the aims of this work by engaging students in meaningful tasks, facilitating significant faculty-student and student-client interactions, giving students frequent performance feedback, and providing opportunities for authentic connections with faculty and diverse groups. As a result, our students leave our program not only learning about families but also ready to help them through various family life education settings.

References

Adams, R. A., Dollahite, D. C., Gilbert, K. R., & Keim, R. E. (1998). *National Council on Family Relations: Ethical principles and guidelines for family scientists*. Retrieved from http://www.ncfr.org/about/board-and-governance/governance/ncfr-ethical-guidelines

Arcus, M. E. (1993). Looking ahead in family life education. In M. E. Arcus, J. D. Schvaneveldt, & J. J. Moss (Eds.), *Handbook of family life education* (Vol. 1, pp. 229–246). Newbury Park, CA: Sage.

Duncan, S. F., & Goddard, H. W. (2011). *Family life education: Principles and practices for effective outreach* (2nd ed.). Thousand Oaks, CA: Sage.

Family Wellness Associates. (2004). *Survival skills for healthy families. Instructor manual, six session video package and couple workbooks*. Scotts Valley, CA: Family Wellness Associates.

Kuh, G. D. (2008). *High-impact educational practices: What they are, who has access to them, and why they matter.* American Association for Colleges & Universities.

Kumpfer, K. L., & DeMarsh, J. P. (1983). *Strengthening families program: Parent training curriculum manual.* Social Research Institute, Graduate School of Social Work, University of Utah.

Powell, L. H., & Cassidy, D. (2007). *Family life education: Working with families across the lifespan* (2nd ed.). Long Grove, IL: Waveland.

Sweet, M., & Michaelsen, L. K. (2012). Critical thinking and engagement: Creative cognitive apprenticeships with team-based learning. In M. Sweet & L. K. Michaelsen (Eds.), *Team based learning in the social sciences and humanities: Group work that works to generate critical thinking and engagement* (pp. 5–32). Sterling, VA: Stylus.

Vazin, T., & Reile, P. (2006). Collaborative learning: Maximizing students' potential for success. In W. Buskist & S. F. Davis (Eds.), *Handbook of the teaching of psychology* (pp. 65–69). Malden, MA: Blackwell.

PART II

Service Learning and Community-Based Experiences

CHAPTER 10

Community-Based Learning with Young Children in a Child Development Center

Mary A. Sciaraffa

Research has shown that a well-educated workforce and competitive compensation structure for early childhood professionals ensures positive outcomes for children (Whitebook & Ryan, 2011). Individuals working with young children and their families need educational preparation and experience in child development, observation methods, early learning environments, developmentally and culturally appropriate practice, and family and community engagement strategies.

This chapter will discuss course components aligned with four High-Impact Practices (Kuh, 2008), the National Association for the Education of Young Children Standards for Early Childhood Professional Preparation (NAEYC, 2009a), and the National Council for Family Relations Certified Family Life Educator Framework for Best Practices in Family Life Education (NCFR, 2011).

10.1 Background Information

For the purposes of this chapter, the term students will refer to adult undergraduate students and the terms child/children will refer to the children enrolled at the university preschool laboratory (hereafter called

M.A. Sciaraffa (✉)
Child and Family Studies, Eastern Kentucky University, Richmond, KY, USA

"preschool lab" or "lab"). The lead teacher on staff is responsible for the children's daily lessons, models good teaching practices, and mentors the adult students. The supervising teacher or instructor refers to the college/university supervisor who teaches the two adult courses, supervises, mentors, and serves as a resource to both the lead teacher and adult students.

This chapter will focus on two different courses, Child Development and Environments for Young Children. The Child Development course is not dependent upon the second course; however, it is a pre-requisite for it. Thus, students can take the Child Development course without taking the other, but they must take the Child Development course before taking the Environments for Young Children course.

Both courses require a laboratory component, which utilizes the theory-practice-reflection process to connect child development and family science theory to actual practice. Student field experiences are conducted at the university preschool lab, housed under the Child and Family Studies academic program, and at the university child development center, housed under the university's student affairs office. Students are engaged in tasks at the university preschool lab as a means designed by the instructor for the student to construct deeper meaning of class lectures to strengthen the knowledge being transferred from the instructor to the student (Gordon & Browne, 2004). Students from both courses engage in multiple levels of education relating to child development, observation methods, early learning environments, developmentally and culturally appropriate practices, and family and community engagement strategies. Planned experiences for both courses are interrelated, thus utilizing all four high-impact practices (Kuh, 2008) discussed within this chapter.

10.1.1 Child Development Course

Students in the Child Development course are involved in active learning via team-based assignments and individual writing, culminating in a cooperative project of a child's portfolio. Students conduct observations at the university preschool lab and engage in discourse to analyze their experiences as it relates to child development theories and pedagogical principles during the class scheduled lecture. Students are asked to actively engage in reflection of child development theory and principles, class discussions, and personal observations. These reflections are translated into a professionally written narrative report. This course provides students with opportunities to integrate, synthesize, and apply knowledge which is essential to deep, meaningful learning experiences.

10.1.2 *Environments for Young Children Course*

In the Environments for Young Children course, a capstone class, students are involved in experiential learning through direct work experience in a university preschool lab. The practicum experiences are an extension of the lab observations from the aforementioned course. In the practicum, students learn to interact with families and put into action the lessons of diversity, family stressors, and family resiliency. Students are expected to apply principles of child development and pedagogy learned in the previously mentioned course. The students develop an Environment Plan, make a Curriculum Project, and implement both with the children in the lab.

10.2 Faculty and Student Peers Interact About Substantive Matters

Student engagement through interactions with faculty, staff, and peers about substantive matter is implemented throughout both courses. The discussions, both formal and informal, and activities surrounding the intellectual content in both courses are intentionally designed to assist students in reflecting on the dialogue and activities to understand their relevance as observed via real-world experiences in the lab. Additionally, students are encouraged by the instructor to continually ask questions of themselves, the faculty, staff at the lab, and their peers as to engage in ongoing dialogue about substantive matters. Individuals who work with young children and their families need to demonstrate an understanding of specific intellectual content which is supported by both the National Association for the Education of Young Children (NAEYC) and the National Council for Family Relations (NCFR). Throughout both courses, students are provided with an academic environment, including experiential activities, to develop a greater understanding of the following:

- Early childhood is a unique and critical stage of life.
- Programs and services for young children must address the *whole child* including social, emotional, cognitive, physical, and language development through a multifaceted delivery system.
- Every child will reach his/her developmental milestones at different rates and therefore programs and services need to be designed to meet the unique needs of individual children and their families.

- Curriculum and activities for children must engage each child in learning that is relevant and meaningful.
- Authentic assessment must be used to not only measure a child's development but also to inform decisions regarding services provided to the child and to the family.

The following sections will describe class activities, course assignments, and lab observations integrate the specific intellectual content through faculty and student peer interactions in the two courses. The topics and activities are designed to be educationally purposeful in increasing dialogue, both in and out of class, increasing the student's investment in time and effort in attending the class and carrying out the activities, and to increase the student's level of reflection to integrate theory, knowledge, and practice. The interactions described in this section go beyond review of material and question and answer types of activities and assignments. The intent of the two courses is to be an ongoing relationship between the instructor and the students and the students with each other to continually discuss and reflect upon the specific intellectual content.

10.3 NAEYC Code of Ethics and Developmentally Appropriate Practice

The NAEYC Code of Ethics (NAEYC, 2005) offers individuals working with young children guidelines for responsible behavior. Students are introduced to this shared code of ethics and encouraged to use it as a common basis for resolving daily decisions. The instructor begins with a class discussion of the core values as it relates to defining key dispositions of an individual who works with young children and their families. Students participate in a self-assessment to determine personal dispositions. Additionally, students are provided with sample ethical dilemmas to work in pairs to resolve using the NAEYC code of Ethics.

Next, students need to understand the elements of NAEYC Developmentally Appropriate Practice (DAP) and the connection to evidence-based practices with young children and families. Truly developmentally appropriate practices take into account a wide variety of skill development within a certain age group and also reflect a thorough understanding of individual temperament, family values, and culture. The instructor repeatedly discusses this topic and points out key elements of

DAP as observed by the students at the preschool lab. Whole group discussions occur during the weekly lectures to assist students in understanding how DAP is utilized in the observed practice at the lab. Additionally, impromptu discussions occur at the lab during the student's observation hour. This allows the instructor to take advantage of the student's "teachable moment" and answer any questions or respond to student's comments immediately, thus strengthening the relationship between the student and faculty and the students getting to know the instructor and peers through meaningful course-related dialogue.

Beginning the initial class meetings with a discussion of the NAEYC Code of Ethics sets the tone for expectations of the student's behaviors as they move to become professionals and as they engage in activities at the lab school. Faculty and students discuss DAP at length throughout the course because many individuals, who have not studied the NAEYC defined term, often misuse it. For example, families hear the term, DAP, from their child's teacher but may not fully understand the depth as defined by NAEYC and misuse the term when speaking to others. The student, as a future professional in the family science field, must fully understand how to first reflect on each child's developmental stage, chronological age, temperament, learning styles, needs and desires, and family culture and traditions before planning a family service plan. Thus, having the faculty and students interact at length to discuss and dissect the Code of Ethics and the term DAP is imperative for the students as future professionals and advocates for evidence-based practices for families and young children. Coupling classroom discussions of the NAEYC Code of Ethics and DAP with supervised observations in the preschool lab, allows students to discover the relevance of the Code of Ethics and the term DAP through real-world experiences.

10.4 Understanding Child Development

Understanding Child Development is a core component of working with young children and their families for the professional requirements of both NAEYC and NCFR. Individuals who work with young children need a solid knowledge base in child development theories and family systems theories, thus the instructor lectures on these topics during class weekly. The instructor includes class activities, such as asking the students to match developmental stages to chronological ages, to deepen the understanding of the theories, principles of development, and stages of development.

Individuals also need to be able to link concepts with practical application. Additional class activities include watching short video clips about development and care of young children. The students are asked to note theoretical concepts discussed or seen within the video. The instructor and students discuss the video clips and the theoretical concepts that link to the applications discussed in the video.

Research indicates that linkages between theoretical concepts and application can be provided to students with supervised experiences and assignments (Grossman & Williston, 2001). More specifically, involving direct observations of early childhood strategies, discussions with professionals, and engaging in relatively brief, supervised interactions within the preschool lab setting contributes to student's abilities to understand the link between theory and practice (Grossman & Williston, 2001). Students, who have focused observation activities and time to debrief in class regarding what was observed, are assisted in making solid connections (Grossman & Williston, 2001). Knowing what is typical child development at each age and stage of early childhood is critical in assisting individuals who work with young children to decide which experiences are most beneficial for children's learning and development. Observations of children's play and interactions with others, assists individuals in learning about specific children and their individual interests, abilities, and developmental progress. The instructor provides the students with an Early Learning and Development Standards checklist that is aligned with the state's Department of Early Care and Education Early Learning and Development Standards. The checklist is divided into developmental domains, thus allowing students to focus their observations on academic skills that are embedded within developmental domains. Students need to have a firm grasp of basic child development to develop appropriate programs and strategies to assist families.

Students spend considerable time in small groups discussing child development theory, child development principles, and the observations conducted at the preschool lab. In class, students practice coding anecdotal records to identify specific developmental domains, stages of development, and children's academic skills. First, students are asked to code the anecdotal record individually, then in pairs as a means to make a solid connection between observing children and understanding children's behaviors and developmental progress.

During the semester, children's progression in developmental domains, stages of development, and children's academic skills are observed by the students and recorded. This information is then discussed in class via lectures, whole group, and small group discussions to connect theory and practice. The instructor of the course is also a teacher at the preschool lab, thus she is able to facilitate an in-depth discussion with the students linking theory to practice because she is fully aware of the events that transpired at the preschool lab. Students are provided with class time to discuss their observations with their small group. Information is then used by the student to complete their own anecdotal records and a narrative report of a specific child. Because the students observe the children all semester, whole group and small group discussions take place during class time each week throughout the semester.

Child development is a combination of several human development theories, such as maturational, psychoanalytic, psychosocial, cognitive-developmental, behaviorism and social learning, bioecological, and essential needs. Ensuring that students are well versed in how these theories link to research and pedagogical practices of working with young children and their families is paramount for instructors to prepare future family science professionals. The instructor ensures the students comprehend theoretical knowledge by continually engaging the students in theoretical discourse and pointing out real-world examples of the theory in practice when the students are observing at the lab. The instructor strives to encourage students to engage in discourse with her and other students regarding children's growth and development. Students are asked to reflect on the discourse and to draw their own conclusions regarding theoretical contributions to child development research and practices in the field. Additionally, the instructor continuously reminds students that it is difficult to understand and explain child growth and development from one single theoretical lens because child development is complex with interactions impacted by both biological and environmental characteristics.

10.5 Understanding the Importance of the Environment

Prior to the children beginning the academic year at the lab, students in the Environments for Young Children course are provided with an intense orientation, which includes in-depth discussions and role-playing. Students learn about the value of the environment, both physical and socio-emotional, and its crucial role in the learning/teaching process. Students learn about health and safety standards, communication strategies, positive guidance techniques, and how to engage children in activities before having direct interaction with the children in the lab. During the semester, students learn about each learning center at the lab via the textbook and weekly lectures. At the end of the week, students are provided with class time to reflect and discuss within a small group the pros and cons of the room arrangement and the chosen children's activities for the week.

Individuals who work with young children and their families need to understand how children's development is impacted by both biological and environmental characteristics. Children's growth and development are influenced by both the child's unique genetic design and the child's experiences encountered within the environment. When faculty and student peers interact about these substantive matters, the student can begin to understand the interplay of both biological and environmental characteristics. Students gain a firm understanding of the expected norms, which is useful in screening and assessing children's developmental progress. Understanding developmental sequences in children's growth and development assists students, future professionals, in using factual information on how to think about children, interact with children, and plan activities for children at various chronological ages and developmental stages. Equipped with a firm understanding of the NAEYC Code of Ethics, Developmentally Appropriate Practice, Child Development, and the importance of the environment, students will be able to explain how an adult responds to a young child with words, direct and indirect actions, gestures, and emotions that are critical to the child's development, thus laying a solid foundation for students to work professionally with young children and their families in developing a family service plan in any number of settings.

10.6 Students Spend Considerable Amounts of Time on Meaningful Tasks

Enhancing the student's learning experience through meaningful tasks assists in strengthening the foundation of student's professional skills. The two aforementioned courses have been intentionally designed to engage students by spending considerable amounts of time on meaningful tasks, thus increasing student's learning and personal development. Meaningful tasks motivate students to invest time and effort in attending class and lab and completing activities. The following activities are designed to build upon one another with each task becoming part of a larger assignment. The assignments are also designed to be educationally purposeful to equip students with transferrable skills that are beneficial to all individuals who work with young children and families within a variety of settings.

10.7 Observing with Objectivity

Students need to understand the difference between watching and observing with objectivity. Students in the Child Development course are required to spend ten hours (one hour per week) observing young children. Three hours are focused on infants and toddlers. These observations are conducted at the university's child development center. Seven hours are focused on preschool children at the university preschool lab. Grossman and Williston (2001) assert participant observation assignments promote reflective thinking, which requires students to observe, record, interpret, and evaluate behaviors of children, teachers, and themselves.

The Child Development students learn about the importance of authentic assessment and develop a portfolio on an assigned child (refer to appendix). The portfolio is assigned as a group project that allows students to work collaboratively to consider different points of view and work with others to support a shared purpose or goal. These skills are necessary as either an early childhood educator or a case manager.

The contents of the assigned child's portfolio include the following:

- child background information;
- report on the family interview;
- anecdotal records;
- visual documentation;
- child work samples; and
- a narrative report of the child's progress (refer to appendix).

The child's background information is provided to the student by the staff of the preschool lab. Students obtain additional information through the parent interview that cannot be obtained through observing the child at the preschool lab. For example, the student may ask the family if the child is able to brush his/her own teeth to ascertain the child's hygiene habits. NAEYC (2013) maintains,

We must make an effort to get to know the children's families and learn about the values, expectations, and factors that shape their lives at home and in their communities. This background information helps us provide meaningful, relevant, and respectful learning experiences for each child and family. (Three core considerations of DAP section, para. 3)

Students are encouraged to take notes on observed events at the preschool lab. This transferrable skill will assist students as they move into the professional role and conduct family interviews and home visits, and then translate the information into a report. The phrases the students capture contribute to the student's learning when they review the notes and reflect on the observed events before they write any report.

The instructor advises students to capture the action in phrases, not complete sentences, and use abbreviations wherever possible. Students should concentrate on the description in order to transfer the notes to anecdotal records, short factual reports that describe a significant event that was observed, for the child's portfolio.

Careful observation of what is actually happening can prevent radical interpretations such as, "Tommy is such an aggressive child." He might be aggressive today, but may usually be friendly on other days. There are many reasons for a child's behavior and objective observation is one of the best ways to find a basis for understanding behavior.

The child communicates through facial expressions, body movements, eyes, language, tone of voice, running, jumping, and wandering. What the child does and how it is done can reveal the child's interests and inner feelings. When a student can understand a child's behavior from the child's point of view and a theoretical lens, the student is moving in the direction of becoming a skilled observer via a real-world experience through a meaningful task. Being a skilled and objective observer who understands behaviors, interests, and inner feelings is invaluable to students as they move into a professional role in the field of family science. However, becoming a skilled and objective observer requires many hours of practice. The instructor works closely with the student and provides frequent feedback to ensure the student's observation skills are being honed over the course of the semester.

Additionally, students are expected to take photographs and video of the child while conducting their observations. These visual documentations serve as another means to engage the students in reflective practice. The student must decide if the observed event is valuable as a visual document and important enough to be placed in the child's portfolio. Students are encouraged to reflect using the following questions from The Portfolio Book (Grace & Shores, 1998):

- What was happening when I took this photograph?
- What happened just before? Just after?
- Who was present?
- Was the activity planned by an adult or did the child engage in a spontaneous activity?
- What kind of learning was happening here—cognitive, social-emotional, or physical development?
- Do the expressions on the child's face reveal insight into the child's disposition or feeling? If so, why?
- Was this a milestone for the child?
- Does this photograph reveal anything about how I believe children learn?
- Does this photograph document what I expected it to? Does the photograph document more than I expected it to?

To assess the child's progression through developmental domains and stages, students use children's work samples. For example, the student needs to understand the stages of writing as it pertains to the developmental domain of physical development and cognitive development. The student needs to collect work samples that demonstrate the child's progression through the stages of writing.

The students individually complete a narrative report that is included in the portfolio (see appendix). Writing a narrative report involves the student systematically reviewing the contents of the portfolio and correlating the observed children's activities to extrinsic standards. Narrative reports do not have to be lengthy, but they should be thorough. A good report contains a summary, with specific examples, of the child's growth, development, and academic achievements.

When students are engaged in the naturalist approach, they are intentionally taking the time to notice what is happening around them, questioning what is happening, and learning to link familiar children's behaviors and activities with theories, developmental characteristics, and pedagogical practices. This does require reflection, either in a discussion with the instructor, lab staff, student peers, children's families, or in written observations. This reflection can provide richness to conversations and documentations as it relates to children's growth and learning. Information can be translated into information for the child's portfolio. Mentally making connections to the theories, developmental characteristics, and pedagogical practices, reflecting on the connections, and documenting the connections from a naturalist approach result in authentic assessments of children's developmental progress. Students work with the instructor and lab staff to use the assessment information to plan developmentally and culturally appropriate activities for children.

10.8 Planning the Environment

Students in the Environments for Young Children course are required to reflect on the intellectual content learned in the Child Development course. The instructor intentionally makes the students think about how the intellectual content and activities from the Child Development course contributed to the experiences the students have in the preschool lab. Then, the instructor assists the students in making the connection that just as meaningful experiences are planned for the adult students, so are meaningful experiences planned for the children. The students are then expected to synthesize the information learned in the Child Development course and in the currently enrolled course to design an Environmental Plan and Curriculum Project for the children at the lab. Thus, providing another meaningful experience for the adults and facilitating reflective practice of intellectual content previously learned.

Students are assigned on a rotating basis to engage children in a specific learning center (e.g., science, math, blocks, dramatic play, music). Students are responsible for developing and implementing an Environment Plan and Curriculum Project which is divided into four parts:

- Lesson plan for an assigned learning center.
- An in-depth lesson to be carried out by the student and observed by the lead teacher.
- Curriculum project product: a non-consumable, student-made item to be used in conjunction with the in-depth lesson.
- Description of curriculum project, including materials for construction and sketch of finished product.

Each student meets twice with the lead teacher to discuss the project. The initial meeting involves the student bringing a rough draft of all the components of the project to discuss feasibility. The student is provided with feedback on the initial rough draft. At this meeting, the student is also made aware of any pertinent resources that would be helpful in the development of the project. The student is instructed to rework the initial draft and meet a second time. During the second meeting, the student is provided with more in-depth feedback regarding the proposed project. The student is advised to use the feedback to finalize the proposed project. The final project is turned in and the student sets up the area, implements the children's lesson, and puts away the materials at the close of the week. The lead teacher grades the final project and the implementation of the lesson. Students meet as a whole group at the end of each week to discuss the children's reactions to the environment and lessons. The instructor, lead teacher, and students discuss strategies to change the environment and adult interactions based upon the children's individual and group needs.

Engaging students through meaningful tasks such as learning to observe objectively, document developmentally progress, and planning the children's environment deepens students understanding of how to put theory into practice. The activities described are designed to increase student's interest and investment in learning and understanding theoretical background, developmental characteristics, and evidence-based practice with young children and their families. Students who understand the cycle of observation, documentation, assessment, and planning are better able to serve their clients in the future because the student is experienced and competent in employing the process to develop family service plans that are relevant to the family's needs as the needs continually change across time.

Students, in both courses, work in close proximity with the instructor and lead teacher during the field experiences in completing their assignments. Moreover, the instructor has deliberately set aside class time for students to work on group assignments. This time allows the instructor and lead teacher to be available to students as questions arise or if they need assistance in other ways, such as brainstorming or talking through an idea. Students are guided and provided with performance feedback in real time as they are working on meaningful tasks during class time. Guidance and feedback is provided to the students from the instructor, the lead teacher, and peer students.

10.9 Students Receive Frequent Performance Feedback

Student assessment involves the instructor looking at information from multiple sources gathered over time before drawing conclusion about a student's progress. Measuring a student's learning across time is an important part of a high-impact program. Accurate and timely assessment, along with data collection (e.g., informal conversations, formal tests, performance on assignments, performance evaluation sheets) and analysis (e.g., attendance, grades, quality of performance in written work and experiential work), is essential for identifying student's needs, making instructional decisions, monitoring progress toward goals, identifying students who may need additional services and supports, and evaluating the overall effectiveness of the course. When instructors make opportunities to provide performance feedback to their students, they can help students understand their strengths and areas for improvement. This next section will discuss various ways for instructors to assess student performance and share the information with their students, as it pertains to the two courses being discussed in this chapter.

The instructor, lead teacher, and students are continually engaged in the process of collaborative inquiry through reflective practice. Students are asked to connect what they observed the children doing or what they do with children to the way they are guided and supported in their own intellectual growth throughout the course (see appendix). This provides students with a framework to be intentional and systematic in gaining insights into their own learning process and new knowledge. Additionally, this assists students in connecting theory to practice (Bullough & Gitlin, 2001).

In both courses, students receive frequent performance feedback. In the Child Development course, students are provided with specific comments on the anecdotal rough drafts. For the narrative reports, students are provided with a rubric (see appendix) that delineates the requirements of the assignment. The instructor uses the rubric to provide detailed feedback to the student on the narrative report rough draft. The student is then encouraged to use the comments to complete final drafts of the anecdotal record and narrative report.

In the Environments for Young Children course, the supervising teacher uses a clinical model of supervision. First, a pre-observation conference is conducted with the whole class to discuss the expectations and evaluations of the student's behaviors during his/her enrollment in the course. Students are provided with a student handbook and a formative evaluation sheet with corresponding categories (see appendix). Students are assessed in each of the following broad categories, which are outlined in detail in subcategories in the student handbook:

- presentation of self;
- interaction with team;
- lab knowledge;
- interaction with staff; and
- interaction with children.

Next, the students are observed by the supervising teacher and the lead teacher. At the beginning of the course, the students are observed for approximately two weeks, but are not graded. The students are coached and mentored during these weeks with a weekly debriefing of the whole class. After the initial probationary period, the students are observed by the supervising teacher and the lead teacher and provided with a summary and analysis. A formative evaluation sheet (see appendix) with each of the above-mentioned broad categories and subcategories is used to provide the student with constructive feedback.

The students are then provided with a time to conduct a post-observation conference with the supervising teacher. The student is encouraged to conduct a post-observation conference analysis to reflect on strengths and areas of improvement. At the end of the course, the students engage in self-analysis as it pertains to their professional growth over the duration of the course. Each student rates him/herself and submits a summative evaluation form (see appendix).

Students in the Environments for Young Children course have to learn how to establish boundaries and negotiate their responsibilities with lab staff, fellow classmates, children, and families in the lab setting. The experiences in the lab provide students with a safe and supportive atmosphere to encounter and work through all of the necessary learning concepts as outlined within the Interpersonal Relationships content area of the NCFR CFLE Framework (NCFR, 2011).

As previously mentioned, student assessment throughout the two courses is ongoing. This allows the instructor and the student to monitor progress. This also allows the instructor to determine instructional needs of the student and provide instructional supports as needed for individual students. Providing students with performance feedback in a "controlled" environment, such as the preschool lab, assists students in learning to utilize the feedback to improve performance. This allows them to be reflective, intentional, and purposeful about professional attitudes and behaviors. Many lessons, planned or not, are learned by students in the Child Development course and the Environments for Young Children course. The overarching lesson is learning to interact with families and putting into action the lessons of diversity, family stressors, family resiliency, family dynamics, and several other courses taught throughout the family science program curriculum. Students begin to understand how to synthesize and integrate information from their other courses and translate intellectual content from family sciences into real-world practice with young children, families, supervisors, and colleagues.

10.10 ACTIVITIES HAVE APPLICATIONS TO DIFFERENT SETTINGS ON/OFF CAMPUS

The activities discussed throughout this chapter have applications to different settings on and off campus. The skills needed by a twenty-first-century employee are similar, yet uniquely different than generations past. Due to the experiential nature and intentional assignments, students will be equipped with transferrable skills such as demonstrating critical thinking, communicating effectively, and working collaboratively.

Students who obtain valuable transferrable skills are more likely to be successful in the workforce and in their work with children and families. Through the two courses described in this chapter, students obtain an understanding of the importance of objectively observing a child's behavior or a social interaction. This skill is necessary for case managers who need to fully understand the child's developmental stage, behavior, and dynamics of social interactions. Through these two courses, students can comprehend reciprocal influences on the family and develop programs that support individuals and families (NCFR, 2011). Case managers must also be able to communicate effectively and write object reports, such as the students in the Child Development course. Additionally, caseworkers must be able to objectively observe the situation and decide on a course of action, as do the students in the Environments for Young Children who observe the children and plan the environment based upon the child's individual needs.

Students in the Child Development course conduct a family interview, thus providing them with an experience similar to a caseworker conducting a family intake interview. Through the work with the lab staff, children, and families, students gain a better understanding of how to engage participants and stakeholders to enhance educational effectiveness (NCFR, 2011).

Students in the Environments for Young Children course are better equipped to plan activities, programs, and services for young children and their family because of their understanding of Developmentally Appropriate Practices (NAEYC, 2009b). This understanding assists the student in applying age appropriate principles of teaching, structuring cognitive content in sequential steps, and honoring learning style preferences (NCFR, 2011). These students are equipped with the skills to evaluate materials, participant's progress, and program effectiveness (NCFR, 2011).

These students have been observed and mentored by professionals in the field who coached them to provide an emotionally supportive environment for young children. Thus, providing the students with critical skills in communication strategies, using positive guidance techniques, and engaging children. Students are expected to apply principles of pedagogy and use a variety of educational techniques (NCFR, 2011). These students will be able to use these skills as early childhood educators, case managers, parent educators, cooperative extension specialists, children's ministers, and other careers that involve working with young children and families.

10.11 Final Thoughts

This chapter has discussed course components aligned with four High-Impact Practices (Kuh, 2008), the National Association for the Education of Young Children Standards for Early Childhood Professional Preparation (NAEYC, 2009a), and the National Council for Family Relations Certified Family Life Educator Framework for Best Practices in Family Life Education (NCFR, 2011).

Student engagement can increase student's learning and personal development. Several examples to engage students in a Child Development course and a practicum, Environments for Young Children, have been discussed. Intellectual content and activities of both courses were educationally purposely designed to:

- put students in deliberate circumstances that essentially demand they interact with faculty and peers about substantive matters;
- engage students in meaningful tasks and provide considerable amounts of time, both inside and outside of class, for students to complete the tasks;
- have instructors remain in close proximity of the student to evaluate and discuss the student's performance with him/her, both formally and informally, in a multitude of ways across time; and
- provide students with an integration of experiential and classroom learning that has applications to different settings on/off campus.

Individuals work with children in various settings. Despite the setting, it is important for individuals to obtain educational preparation and field experience in child development, observation methods, early learning environments, developmentally and culturally appropriate practice, and family and community engagement strategies. Through course work and supervised field experiences, whether conducted at a campus-based children's center or within a community center, students can obtain a solid understanding of the linkages between theory, pedagogical principles, and practice.

REFERENCES

Bullough, R. V., & Gitlin, A.d. (2001). *Becoming a student of teaching: Linking knowledge production and practice* (2d ed.). New York: Routledge Falmer.

Gordon, A., & Browne, K. (2004). *Beginnings and beyond: Foundations in early childhood education.* New York: Delmar.

Grace, C., & Shores, E. (1998). *The portfolio book: A step-by-step guide for teachers.* Lewisville, NC: Gryphon House.

Grossman, S., & Williston, J. (2001). Strategies for teaching early childhood students to connect reflective thinking to practice. *Childhood Education, 77,* 236–240.

Kuh, G. (2008). *High-impact educational practices: What they are, who has access to them, and why they matter.* Retrieved from http://www.neasc.org/downloads/aacu_high_impact_2008_final.pdf

National Association for the Education of Young Children. (2005). *Code of Ethical Conduct and Statement of Commitment.* Retrieved from http://www.naeyc.org/positionstatements/ethical_conduct

National Association for the Education of Young Children. (2009a). *NAEYC Standards for Early Childhood Professional Preparation.* Retrieved from http://www.naeyc.org/positionstatements/prepstds

National Association for the Education of Young Children. (2009b). *Position Statement on Developmentally Appropriate Practice.* Retrieved from http://www.naeyc.org/positionstatements/dap

National Association for the Education of Young Children. (2013). *Developmentally Appropriate Practice.* Retrieved from http://www.naeyc.org/DAP

National Council on Family Relations. (2011). *Family Life Education Framework Poster and PowerPoint—Third Edition.* Retrieved from http://www.ncfr.org

Whitebook, M., & Ryan, S. (2011). Degrees in context: Asking the right questions about preparing skilled and effective teachers of young children. *NIEER Policy Brief* (Issue 22, April 2011). New Brunswick, NJ: National Institute for Early Education Research.

CHAPTER 11

Family Life Education with Diverse Community Partners

Jonathan Davis, Celeste Hill, and Kristie Chandler

11.1 Overview of Implementation

Our Family Life Education (FLE) course is two semester hours, and it was reshaped eight years ago into a service-learning course that engages several community partners annually. Incorporating service-learning was an excellent choice for this course because students consistently struggled with motivation in FLE in previous semesters. Sometimes they became disinterested because the course emphasized public speaking skills that already are strengths of their Samford education. Other times students found little inspiration in a contrived (e.g., classroom, dorm, sorority) setting. The redesigned course transformed students' motivation as they connected with actual community needs, and they were thus required and expected to provide professional-level education. This outcome was consistent with research on service-learning and engagement of students in the classroom experience (Astin, Vogelgesang, Ikeda, & Yee, 2000). We also discovered four additional benefits that are consistent with high-impact practices.

J. Davis (✉) • C. Hill • K. Chandler
Department of Human Development and Family Life Education,
Samford University, Birmingham, AL, USA

First, students learned about the importance of flexibility and communication in collaborative relationships. This flexibility is modeled by the instructors in-course assignments via flexible project-based due dates that depend upon when the project can realistically be accomplished at the community partner's site. And, flexibility is extended to relationships with community partners, who often provide services every day of the year and don't fit neatly into a semester-by-semester calendar. The community partners also show flexibility in offering training to our students; as an example, they might provide training and orientation for our students at a special time, or waive their normal requirement that volunteers commit to the organization for an entire year.

> "Why would a homeless person waste so much money buying cigarettes?!"—*opportunity for modeling and teaching skilled dialogue*

Flexibility, however, does not extend to altering the purpose of our course or our community partner's mission. The boundaries of flexibility are clarified in communication during the planning phase of the course and throughout the implementation (see below).

The central importance of communication is obvious to the students throughout the course. This lesson is also both experiential and didactic: students might encounter community partners who don't return emails, or they discover that their expectations about a project are disappointed after misunderstandings of roles. Sometimes students witness miscommunication within a community partner's agency that also provides a valuable glimpse into the often frenetic world of small nonprofits.

Second, students gain familiarity with skilled dialogue (Barrera & Kramer, 2009; Duncan & Goddard, 2012) to facilitate communication with diverse others. In our view, the related high-impact practice (i.e., experience with diverse others) must be accompanied by guidance and deliberate attention to avoid unintentional consequences (e.g., reifying students' prejudices). We provide the needed guidance and attention via other high-impact practices: classroom discussions about aspects of the students' experiences that are surprising, frustrating, or confusing. We frame these sensations as signals of an opportunity for learning.

Often, such opportunities cause us to reflect on the key aspects of skilled dialogue—respect, reciprocity, and responsiveness (Barrera & Kramer, 2009; Duncan & Goddard, 2012). This kind of dialogue is modeled by community partners when they initially attend the regular class time to describe their agency and purpose (see below). And, instructors model skilled dialogue in their interactions with community partners and students.

Third, we find that a significant benefit of engaging the community is our students' strengthened network of relationships within the social service community. This higher-order learning occurs indirectly as we discuss obstacles to collaboration with the various partners, and as students learn from other students' experiences.

Fourth, students gain proficiency in a simple and powerful model for providing workshops (Brooks-Harris & Stock-Ward, 1999) that students can use in any setting. (High-impact practice—Kuh, 2008: Activities have applications to different settings on/off campus.)

With these benefits in mind, we present some guiding principles for course design and key methods for implementation. Readers also may be interested in our course objectives, displayed in Fig. 11.1.

11.2 Guiding Principles and Practices

This section describes how we establish relationships within this teaching triangle composed of instructor, students, and community partner.

> "We showed up on time but there was nobody to greet us ~ we weren't expected!"—*typical remark reflecting communication challenges*

11.2.1 Cultivating Community Partners

First, we dedicate time in the prior term creating partnerships with community organizations, based upon discerning their authentic needs for student assistance. This groundwork laid by the instructor also reflects skilled dialogue. Rather than focusing on simply getting any partner for the course, the instructor cultivates genuine curiosity about the potential partners' needs and assesses whether students can realistically help with an educational presentation.

Partnerships often begin with an initial phone call or email from the instructor, requesting a time to meet and discuss potential collaboration. If the community agency agrees, the instructor will go to the community site and seek to understand the mission and needs of the community organization, as well as any constraints (e.g., scheduling) that are likely to become challenges. The instructor brings along a copy of the course syllabus and schedule, and a contract to establish supervisory responsibility

> By the end of our 16-week term, students will have:
>
> 1. Designed, administered, compiled, and analyzed an assessment of specific family life skills, knowledge, and/or attitudes needed by a target audience.
> 2. Designed a two-hour (minimum) family life education program using foundational family life education planning and design practices.
> 3. Team-taught a family life education program to a group of adult learners.
> 4. Evaluated the content and process of the teaching program, and recommended improvements in future programs.
> 5. Demonstrated competence in family life education skills and knowledge.
> 6. Evaluated their family life education skills.
> 7. Collaborated with a community partner involved in family life education to share discipline-specific knowledge and/or skills.
> 8. Developed a sense of ethical practice as a family life educator.
> 9. Articulated understanding of the public benefit of family life education and its congruence with the mission of Samford University.
> 10. Deepened awareness of the role of Family Life Education in the student's vocation and in the community.
> 11. Developed an understanding of the complexity of social issues addressed by Family Life Education.

Fig. 11.1 Course Objectives

with the community partner, and to clarify expectations. If the possibility of students meeting an existing need is clear, and all terms are agreeable, the community partner is invited to attend a class meeting during the second week of the upcoming term to assist in student team formation.

A word of caution—the type of partnership developed with the community partner may be detrimental to the quality of a student's learning experiences. In some cases, the community partner may not understand the role of the student as it relates to their organization. The student may be assigned duties by the community partners that do not foster trusting relationships with the target population. These duties (e.g., sorting clothes in a closet), in turn, may hamper the student's ability to develop and present a program well received by the target population. In other partnerships, the community partner may be experiencing such high levels of turnover that it is difficult for students to maintain a working relationship with those responsible for scheduling and monitoring their visits to the facility. In either of these situations, it is difficult for students to develop the relationships necessary for effective implementation of programs.

11.2.2 *Student-Partner Matching*

At the earliest opportunity during the semester, we familiarize students with course requirements and outcomes using teaching plan examples published by the National Council on Family Relations (NCFR). Then we begin building the second key relationships: teams based upon the match between students and our community partners, who attend class as soon as possible after the start of the term. During this class meeting (described as mandatory in the course schedule), each community partner briefly presents the history and mission of the organization, the specific need that an educational presentation can meet, and any constraints (e.g., scheduling). After all of the partner presentations, students are allowed to form groups according to their perception of the best match.

In our experience, sometimes the match is based upon passion or interest in a topic and other times the match is pragmatic. For example, schedule compatibility plays a surprisingly important role in determining teams. We find that it is best to let students self-select for these reasons, because the students are the only ones who can determine how much effort and which particular sacrifices they will need to make to be successful in the course. In rare circumstances, we will encourage students who are ambivalent about their choices to move to a group that might not have enough members, but our community partners have always been able to find a team of 3–5 students on this important day.

11.2.3 *Team Structure and Development*

Developing the student teams and cultivating relationships within the students' teams and between teams and community partners is the third process. We impose a structure on the team that is designed to minimize disruption to the community partner (among other goals). Teams must consist of 3–5 students, and one of the team members gets an hour of credit toward the minimum requirements for functioning as the team coordinator, who manages scheduling and correspondence between the team members and community partner. Some community partners are able to accommodate two or three teams, while others can work successfully with one team only.

Once team formation is accomplished and partnerships are selected, the effort to maintain those relationships sometimes lags or encounters difficulties. In our experience, two difficulties are predictable. First, students may be surprised by the community partner's lack of responsiveness. We use this *trigger feeling* of frustration as a teachable moment—it helps us learn about both the world of nonprofits which may be flooded with volunteers and multiple demands. And, it also helps us learn to communicate our needs in different ways until we have some success.

The second difficulty comes as complaints from students who are overscheduled, and who may have difficulty visiting the community partner the required number of times. These students sometimes encounter conflict between their schooling vs. other commitments, and we have taken specific steps within the curriculum to help minimize these concerns. We provide advanced notice in the prior term, when students register for the course, that this course requires significant travel off-campus. We intentionally schedule the class at a time of day that conflicts with other courses requiring off-campus travel (e.g., internship), so students typically are unable to register for more than one similarly demanding course in the term. And, we use this challenge as a means to convey the real costs of collaboration to students, while simultaneously asserting that the costs are justified by the substantial benefits.

11.3 Detailed Methods

During the Liberal Education and America's Promise (LEAP) campaign, the Association of American Colleges and Universities (2013) developed a set of principles of excellence and identified essential learning outcomes that provide a new framework for college learning in the twenty-first century. George Kuh's (2008) research clarified pedagogical methods leading toward these goals. In addition to the principles and practices mentioned earlier, the methods below describe how we implement three additional high-impact practices described by Kuh (2008).

11.3.1 *Authentic Connections and Time on Task*

One of the key insights we convey about working with people who are different is the essential role of a trusting relationship. We assert that a trusting relationship is necessary for the people we hope to reach to be able to listen to us, and it takes time to form that relationship. So, we emphasize that time with the community partner (i.e., time on task) is correlated with the authentic connection. For these reasons, we require students to meet with their community partners a minimum of seven times, and a minimum of 15 total hours over the term (for a two-hour course).

To enhance connections, it is important for our students to distinguish themselves by these regular visits and by a departmental shirt they wear that brands our collective presence. Many of the people we serve have regular contact with anonymous volunteers, some of whom are mandated by the courts, and we wish to convey that our students are conducting service-learning, more than community service.

To further develop the relationship and focus on connections, we require students to complete a three-part needs assessment. The first part of the assessment involves summarizing attributed needs of the audience based upon students' own preconceptions of the people they are serving, an interview with the community partner staff, and a brief literature review to identify risk and protective factors they might be able to address in their educational presentation.

The second part of the assessment (due later in the term) summarizes factors that might influence students' relationships with their audience and describes the felt needs of the audience, based upon students' interactions with them during visits. The third part of the assessment (near the time of the presentation) is a formal data collection conducted via survey or standardized interview that allows students to clarify the current knowledge of the audience on the learning outcomes they have selected.

11.3.2 *Frequent Performance Feedback*

During the course of the term, students have opportunities to receive feedback at many points on the needs assessment, and from many sources (e.g., the community partners, instructors, and one another). Also, students submit documentation of their progress in accumulating hours by midterm to identify any need for intervention.

To encourage feedback within the teams and commitment to the project by all members, we use a policy that allows students to evaluate one another's contributions to the team. Their average evaluation score determines a multiplier used with all of the team assignments, such that students' grades will not be adversely affected by one student, but rather informed by a combined estimation of their teammates.

11.3.3 Faculty and Student Peers Interact About Substantive Matters

This high-impact practice is best illustrated with a description of the course schedule, because peer and faculty interaction is needed throughout the term as the assignments are developed. First, we require students to meet with their community partner for an orientation during the first three weeks of the term. Following this meeting, they submit a "Who, Where, and When report" describing their target date, setting, and audience for the presentation. This assignment provides them with a deadline that they determine for themselves in consultation with the community partner.

The needs assessment report is submitted next, in three phases over several weeks (see above). A teaching plan based upon the needs assessment is due two weeks to ten days before the scheduled presentation, and we provide class time to allow teams to describe their presentation to one another. This opportunity for feedback and interaction serves several purposes—the students gain confidence in their delivery and in their mastery of the content of the presentation by describing it with peers, and the presentations become higher quality through accessing the creativity and thoughtfulness of the entire class. Also, instructors can use this time to reflect with the entire class on potential pitfalls that might be present in a particular instructional approach or topic.

During the class immediately following the presentation, the instructor asks the team to describe how it went. When the team describes their impressions (e.g., "It went really well!", "The audience was really engaged!"), the instructor requires students to articulate evidence by repeatedly inquiring of the students "How did you know [it went really well]?" and "What told you [the audience was engaged]?"

The instructor also inquires about students' learning objectives and uses this opportunity to remind students about the distinction between process evaluation and outcome evaluation. Students are reminded to use evidence in their outcome evaluation report. The outcome evaluation report also requires students to visit their community partner a final time after the presentation and assess their learning outcomes, formally or informally.

The final assignment of the term, a self-reflection of strengths and growth areas as a family life educator, also requires substantive interaction with peers and the community partner. Students are required to select one team member and ask her or him for input, which provides an opportunity to develop skills in a frank discussion that might not arise during typical teamwork. Students also have a formal evaluation meeting with their community partner, who completes a standard form and provides them with verbal feedback.

References

Association of American Colleges and Universities. (2013). *LEAP: Liberal education and America's promise.* Retrieved from http://www.aacu.org/leap/vision.cfm

Astin, A. W., Vogelgesang, L. J., Ikeda, E. K., & Yee, J. A. (2000). *How service learning affects students. Executive summary.* Los Angeles, CA: Higher Education Research Inst.

Barrera, I., & Kramer, L. (2009). *Using skilled dialogue to transform challenging interactions: Honoring identity, voice, and connection.* Baltimore, MD: Paul H. Brookes Pub. Co.

Brooks-Harris, J. E., & Stock-Ward, S. R. (1999). *Workshops: Designing and facilitating experiential learning.* Thousand Oaks, CA: Sage.

Duncan, S. F., & Goddard, H. W. (2012). *Family life education: Principles and practices for effective outreach* (2nd ed.). Thousand Oaks, CA: Sage.

Kuh, G. (2008). *High-impact educational practices: What they are, who has access to them, and why they matter.* Washington, DC: American Association of Colleges and Universities.

CHAPTER 12

Interprofessional Field-Based Learning in a Program Planning and Evaluation Course for Students in Human Service Programs

Charlene VanLeeuwen

The benefits that can result from undergraduate students and community groups working closely together are many. The Council for the Advancement of Standards in Higher Education (2012) outlines the well-researched benefits to students, faculty, and communities along with a definition of service-learning programs (S-LP), the roles of S-LP, and the critical importance of the fundamental concepts of reflection and reciprocity for effective campus-community partnerships. The course described in this chapter provides students from four different human service programs with the opportunity to develop their skills in developing educational and outreach programs to promote healthy lifestyles for diverse population groups. Students work in interprofessional teams with local human service community organizations for the entire program development process. This includes completing a comprehensive needs assessment, as well as implementing and evaluating a portion of the educational sessions developed for the project.

C. VanLeeuwen (✉)
Department of Applied Human Sciences, University of Prince Edward Island, Charlottetown, PE, Canada

12.1 Strengths and Challenges of an Interprofessional Field-Based Approach to Student Learning

Through working directly with children, youth, newcomers to Canada, seniors and other groups, students learn firsthand the challenges associated with communicating health messages to populations that they are not necessarily familiar with. The ability to apply class learning to real-world situations is one of the key outcomes identified by Brownell and Swaner (2009) in their review of high-impact practices. Students gain valuable real-life experience by working in cooperation with different groups of people to collectively identify their needs and the factors which should be taken into account to develop effective activities geared to their target population. Changing behavior is much more complex than just presenting information. Activities have to support changes in behavior, whether this related to choosing a healthy snack based on food group recommendations for various age groups, how to manage your time as a student or explore strategies for new parents to incorporate physical activity into their day as they adapt to this new role. It is this real-life context that supports deeper learning and broader benefits for students, along with community organizations and the populations they serve.

Studies in a variety of disciplines have found that experiential learning can result in greater academic performance and attendance along with improved self-reflection and self-understanding (e.g. Brownell & Swaner, 2009; Gupta, 2004; Koles, Stolfi, Borges, Nelson, & Parmelee, 2010; Kuh, 2008; Michaelsen, Knight, & Fink, 2002; Rogers & Freiberg, 1994). In one study, it was found that women and older students seem to reap the benefits of team-based learning (Burbach, Matkin, Gambrell, & Harding, 2010). With the vast majority of the students in three of these four programs being female, this would be an added strength to this project. Walton and Baker (2009) found that group projects were an effective means to deliver not only content knowledge, but working on group projects also resulted in improvements in students' communication skills, a critical skill area for students in human service programs such as Family Science. In a recent publication, Swaner (2012) discusses how engaged learning addresses four learning dimensions: that the learning be developmental, holistic, integrative and contextual in promoting interdependence and engagement of students. The student project described further on, touches on each of these dimensions.

From the perspective of our community partners, the opportunity to provide clients with learning opportunities that are outside the usual programs and services that they offer is an attractive option for them. The programs developed may capitalize on areas of expertise that the students may have that staff do not (e.g. the development of a series of food safety sessions for newly arrived refugee clients served through a Canadian Life Skills program). Others have served as a pilot for an extension of family life education programming that is already in place or tap into existing structures where the participants are interested in lifelong learning. A couple of examples would be "Lunch and Learn" sessions prepared for workplace employee support committees or the Seniors' Active Living Centre. The reciprocal nature of these benefits is one aspect which has been emphasized in discussions with students and community partners when establishing new and renewing existing partnerships for the student projects. When human service organizations are pressed for staff time and funds, if we are asking them to work with us to support deeper student learning, there needs to be benefits to the organization in return.

Not everything runs smoothly in using this approach to learning. Challenges that have been identified in the literature are student workload, provision of feedback to enhance collaborative learning, and faculty preparation for effective use of these strategies. Ruiz-Gallardo, Castano, and Gomez-Alday (2011) looked at student workload and outcomes following a shift in teaching style to problem-based and cooperative learning. While they found that marks, dropouts and attendance were markedly improved, student workload was also higher. Anecdotally, this finding appears to be consistent in conversations with students in this course as well. This should serve as a red flag for instructors to consider given our knowledge of the busy lives our students lead.

Provision of constructive and individualized feedback to students is an ongoing challenge in this type of collaborative or team environment. Developing and adapting current pieces of the project to enable instructors to see where an individual student is one of our ongoing activities. Tied very closely to this is finding appropriate mechanisms to provide constructive and individualized formative feedback to students in a timely manner so they can still use the feedback to improve their performance and the project product.

Social loafing (Latané, Williams, & Harkins, 2006) in small group or team environments is sadly one of the realities that our students encounter and, in my teaching experience, one of the most time-consuming issues that student groups encounter. However, the insights and interpersonal problem-solving skills that students can develop as they work through this type of situation with support from the instructor can also provide exceptionally valuable learning at a variety of levels. Griesbaum and Gortz (2010) recently completed a study looking at feedback methods for self- and peer evaluation, finding that these assessments should also be regarded as an instructor tool to provide support for group processes. From an instructor's perspective, this behavior is also problematic, especially when it comes to assigning marks for group activities. Making use of a variety of assessment processes that incorporate both group and individual tasks has been helpful in this regard.

Another challenge is our ability as instructors to change our teaching practice and implement these approaches in our classrooms. Burbach, Matkin, Gambrell, and Harding (2010) found that instructors employing research-supported, classroom-based pedagogies of teamwork positively affect student teamwork outcomes and those students benefit from instructors who are familiar with and practice these approaches. To do this, we need to move into new territory which requires additional time and resources, both of which are often in short supply on university campuses.

12.2 Description of Course

This course provides students from four different human service programs, family science, child and family studies, kinesiology and food and nutritional sciences, with the opportunity to develop their skills in developing educational programs to promote healthy lifestyles for diverse population groups. Students work in interprofessional teams with local human service community organizations for the entire program development process. In addition, they deliver a portion of the program sessions to the intended audience with the support of the instructor and community partner organization and conduct an evaluation of the sessions that have been implemented (Table 12.1).

Table 12.1 Course Objectives

- Understand the theoretical basis and practice of program planning, implementation and evaluation for human service professionals.
- Design, implement and evaluate an educational program for children, youth, adults, families or a specific target population.
- Consider factors and behaviors which challenge the development, delivery and evaluation of community-based education programs.
- Build skills in working with a planning committee.
- Develop expertise in working with stakeholders in a community setting.

12.3 Critical Reading and Integration Tests (CRITs)

Based on team-based learning practices (Sweet & Michaelsen, 2012), students complete five or six in-class tests throughout the semester. The test questions are multiple choice or true/false and are knowledge based, drawing directly from the assigned readings. Critical Reading and Integration Tests (CRITs) are completed following student reading of the assigned material but prior to in-class application activities. Students complete the test individually and then immediately proceed to redo the test with their team. Here they are given ample time to discuss and challenge each other as they come to a consensus for which responses they will select as a team. Once all teams have completed the CRIT, the questions are reviewed immediately with the entire class; however, there is no immediate discussion of the responses. Once the answers have been reviewed, teams have the option to prepare a written appeal. Throughout this process, instructor observations confirm that team discussions are very focused on the assigned reading.

12.4 Program Development, Implementation and Evaluation Project

The major assignment is to plan, implement and evaluate an eight-hour educational program targeted for children, youth, seniors, families or other designated population group. Students work in teams of 6–8 on the project. Student teams and community partner organizations are assigned by the instructors. Team assignment is based on a variety of criteria. Each team will have students from all four academic programs, a relatively equal balance of students that describe themselves as outgoing or more reserved. Students indicate a high degree of comfort in assuming a leadership role in small groups and students on the Dean's list are also distributed among all of the teams. The project is reviewed and approved by the Faculty of Science Research Ethics Board and teams must plan to obtain informed consent from participants or their parent/guardian. The course instructor(s) are supported in community partner liaison tasks by the Field Placement Coordinator.

12.5 Team Presentations

Each team is required to prepare two class presentations. In the first 30-minute presentation, which is scheduled around the midpoint in the semester, teams describe their planning processes to date. They briefly outline the situation and take the class through their problem analysis. This information is incorporated into a clearly articulated rationale for the proposed program which they can then take to decision makers with their community partner organization. The presentation then goes on to share a detailed description of the priority population supported with appropriate evidence including but not limited to recent research studies and government statistics. In the remaining presentation time, students outline the methodology and findings from their comprehensive needs assessment, the program mission statement, with associated goals and objectives and a comprehensive logic model for the proposed program.

The second 45–50-minute presentation takes place at the end of the semester and includes a brief description of the theory of behavior change that the team believes would be effective with the particular population they are working with and an explanation of why this theory was selected. Following this, teams proceed to give a general overview of instructional plans for the program and the educator approach(es) they plan to use and why. Teams are expected to prepare a marketing plan and a detailed budget for the sessions that they implemented. When teams outline their program evaluation, they provide a brief rationale of the evaluation approach deemed appropriate for the program along with their evaluation framework with evaluation questions and indicators as well as further details of the evaluation design, such as how data was collected, analyzed and reported. They also share their evaluation results from all forms of analyses completed as well as their interpretation of these analyses. Presentations wrap up with the team's recommendations for the partner organization concerning this program.

12.6 Team and Individual Activities

Teams complete a series of in-class activities directly associated with the development of their team's program. Feedback includes ad hoc comments during class time as students work on specific in-class activities, formative feedback when activities are submitted (following class time), summative feedback for the two team presentations on the program development processes and two peer evaluations at mid and end of semester.

12.7 Assessment and Evaluation

Critical Reading Integration Tests (CRITs) which are similar to readiness assessment tests in the team-based learning literature are worth 30 % of final mark. This mark is weighted 70 % from individual tests and 30 % from the team tests. This is to recognize that the team presentation marks will be the same for all team members, so this allows an opportunity for students to demonstrate their knowledge on an individual basis. The Program Development Project is worth 70 % of the final mark, made up of marks from the two presentations, each worth 20 % and multiple in-class activities worth a total of 30 %. The in-class activities are a combination of individual and teamwork and include student input on team members' performance via the two peer evaluations.

12.8 Elements of High-Impact Practices

12.8.1 Students Spend Considerable Amounts of Time on Meaningful Tasks

In addition to the CRIT discussions described earlier, students become very engaged and creative as they begin to see how individual in-class application activities related to the course readings help them build sections of their semester-long program development project. In particular, students put significant time and effort into the preparation of their instructional plans. This attention to detail is evident as they take steps to ensure that the activities do not simply meet learning goals. They work hard to develop activities that also meet the broader needs of the intended audience (e.g. developmental needs, literacy levels, comfort level with technology or language interpretation). Students know that they will be using these instructional plans to develop activities for members of the community and this provides added impetus to devote the time and effort needed. They want to be well prepared and well received when they venture out of the classroom and into the community to put these plans into practice.

12.8.2 Faculty and Student Peers Interact over Time About Substantive Matters

Defining the "substantive matters" faculty and students are interacting about presents challenges in interpretation. Looking at definitions of substantive, one sees words such as actual, real-life, essential, with a solid firm, practical basis (Merriam-Webster Dictionary, 2012). Certainly as students and instructors work collaboratively on the program development project, discussions reflect these dimensions of substantive as they focus on real-life issues grounded in practical, evidence-based information and activities.

Throughout this course, discussion with peers is integral to student learning. In addition to CRIT discussions, a substantial portion of class time is dedicated to working with fellow team members on the project over the course of the entire semester. Initially, some teams attempt to divide up the project with each student doing their respective piece. They soon realize that this limits their learning about the program development process very significantly and will leave them at a disadvantage in future situations such as Field Placements or Dietetic Internship placements. The instructor and community liaison model highly collaborative practices in the classroom and provide strong encouragement to student teams to do the same. Some examples include consistently addressing the team as a whole, willingness to meet with teams as a whole outside of class time and ensuring the electronic communication about the project is directed to the team, not just an individual student. During class time, the instructor and community liaison support circulate through the class responding to questions on an ad hoc basis. Based on the depth of the questions, it is evident that students are highly engaged. When working through the structured in-class activities applying some of the more challenging material, such as developing a thorough needs assessment, using the theories of behavior change to develop an educational activity or connecting evaluation questions with the desired program outcomes, teams keep both the instructor(s) and community liaison support staff on their toes posing questions related to how the activity applies to their particular community partner organization, or the intended audience for their program.

12.8.3 Students Experience Diversity Through Contact with People Who Are Different Than Themselves

The diversity that students experience through this project is much broader than cultural or ethnic diversity (see Table 12.2). Through this project, students end up working with different types of organizations, families and individuals at different points in the lifespan, as well as a variety of human service professionals. Assigning teams to work with specific partner organizations is a relatively new practice for our program which has turned out to have several very positive outcomes. By assigning the community organizations, we have been able to ensure that there are greater diversity opportunities for students in all aspects of the project, whether they are experiencing the diversity directly or hearing about another team's experiences during one of the classroom presentations. In addition, the interprofessional mix of students on each team provides chances for students in the four different programs to learn about and value the input and disciplinary perspectives of their peers who are studying in related human service disciplines.

Table 12.2 Diversity Experience by Students

Types of diversity students experienced	Examples
Cultural or ethnic	Acadian or other Francophone minority, Immigrant and refugee Newcomers to Canada, Mi'kmaq (First Nation community)
Individuals, couples or families	Mothers and toddlers group, Canada Games athletes, Teens in a life skills program, Families with preschool age children, Couples over 55
Populations at different points in the lifespan	Young parents, Retired adults, Day camp children
Types of organization	Workplace, Child care facility, NGO, Faith-based organization
Geographic communities served	Urban, rural communities
Work with a variety of human service professionals	Early Childhood Educators, Family Life Educators, Dietitians, Elite level Coaches and Trainers, Social Workers, Occupational Therapists, Elementary and Secondary School teachers, Workplace Wellness Coordinators
Work closely with students in four human service academic programs	Child and Family Studies, Family Science, Food and Nutritional Sciences, Kinesiology

12.8.4 Students Receive Frequent Performance Feedback

Feedback on the in-class activities is primarily formative in nature in the form of constructive comments to support continued progress on individual components of the program and is provided during every class. In addition, written formative feedback is provided for 6–8 key in-class activities, which are a mixture of team and individual assignments, most of which are completed during class time. Summative evaluation comes into play through the two group presentations, the CRITs and the peer evaluations. Presentations and peer evaluations are done at the midterm point and the end of semester, while the six CRITs are distributed throughout the first eight weeks of the semester. As noted earlier, students receive their individual and team CRIT marks by the end of the class period in which they were written.

12.8.5 Activities Have Applications to Different Settings On/Off Campus

Our partnerships with a wide variety of community organizations enable students to see how the activities developed with or for a specific population group can be adapted and applied to other groups or settings. For example, all teams conduct a needs assessment. However, some partners are employers providing training or a service for their employees while another team of students may be working with coaches and athletes on a sports team or another developing a life skills transition program for students considering postsecondary education at a college or university. The process of conducting the needs assessment remains similar despite the wide range of settings.

12.8.6 Authentic Connections Are Made with Peers, Faculty, Community and/or the University

The nature of this project, with everyone working toward the creation of a program that is *needed* and can be used by the participants and the community partner organization, grounds the interactions of student peers, faculty and community organization staff in the practical aspects of program planning and evaluation. While students learn about the program development process, the population to be served and their community partner organization; the partner organization staff is sharing information about their agency and the clients they serve. Once they reach the point of implementing the sessions, interactions are focused around the needs of the participants and the sharing of educational or outreach content. With the overarching goals of developing needed programs that promote healthy lifestyles and decision-making for children, youth, adults, families or specific population groups, the connections between these various groups remain very practical and authentic.

References

Brownell, J. E., & Swaner, L. E. (2009). High-impact practices: Applying the learning outcomes literature to the development of successful campus programs. *Peer Review, Spring 2009.* Washington, DC: American Association of Colleges & Universities.

Burbach, M. E., Matkin, G. S., Gambrell, K. M., & Harding, H. E. (2010). The impact of preparing faculty in the effective use of student teams. *College Student Journal, 44*(3), 752–761.

Council for the Advancement of Standards in Higher Education. (2012). The role of service-learning programs. In *CAS Professional Standards for Higher Education* (8th ed.). Washington, DC: Council for the Advancement of Standards. Retrieved from http://www.cas.edu/getpdf.cfm?PDF=E86EC8E7-9B94-5F5C-9AD22B4FEF375B64

Griesbaum, J., & Gortz, M. (2010). Using feedback to enhance collaborative learning: An exploratory study concerning the added value of self- and peer-assessment by first-year students in a blended learning lecture. *International Journal on E-Learning, 9*(4), 481–503.

Gupta, M. L. (2004). Enhancing student performance through cooperative learning in physical sciences. *Assessment & Evaluation in Higher Education, 29*(1), 63–73.

Koles, P. G., Stolfi, A., Borges, N. J., Nelson, S., & Parmelee, D. X. (2010). The impact of team-based learning on medical students' academic performance. *Academic Medicine: Journal of the Association of American Medical Colleges, 85*(11), 1739–1745.

Kuh, G. (2008). *High-impact educational practices: What they are, who has access to them and why they matter.* Washington, DC: Association of American Colleges and Universities. www.aacu.org.leap

Latané, B., Williams, K., & Harkins, S. (2006). Many hands make light the work: The causes and consequences of social loafing. In J. M. Levine & R. L. Moreland (Eds.), *Small groups* (pp. 297–308). New York, NY: Psychology Press.

Merriam-Webster Dictionary. (2012). *Substantive*. Retrieved from http://www.merriam-webster.com/dictionary/substantive
Michaelsen, L. K., Knight, A. B., & Fink, L. D. (2002). *Team-based learning: A transformative use of small groups.* Westport, CT: Praeger.
Rogers, C. R., & Freiberg, H. J. (1994). *Freedom to learn.* New York, NY: Merrill/Macmillan College Publishing Co.
Ruiz-Gallardo, J., Castano, S., & Gomez-Alday, J. J. (2011). Assessing student workload in problem based learning: Relationships among teaching method, student workload and achievement. A case study in natural sciences. *Teaching and Teacher Education: An International Journal of Research and Studies, 27*(3), 619–627.
Swaner, L. E. (2012). The theories, contexts and multiple pedagogies of engaged learning: What succeeds and why? In D. W. Harward & A. P. Finley (Eds.), *Transforming undergraduate education: Theory that compels and practices that succeed.* Lanham, MD: Rowman and Littlefield.
Sweet, M., & Michaelsen, L. K. (2012). *Team-based learning in the social sciences and humanities: Group work that works to generate critical thinking and engagement.* Sterling, VA: Stylus Publishing.
Walton, K. L. W., & Baker, J. C. (2009). Group projects as a method of promoting student scientific communication and collaboration in a public health microbiology course. *Bioscene: Journal of College Biology Teaching, 35*(2), 16–22.

Supplemental Sources

DeMartino, D. J. (1999). Employing adult education principles in instructional design. *SITE 99: Society for Information Technology & Teacher Education International Conference* (10th, San Antonio, TX, February 28–March 4, 1999).
Kolb, D. A. (1984). Experiential Learning: *Experience as the Source of Learning and Development.* Englewood Cliffs, N.J.: Prentice-Hall, Inc.
Wilson, A. L., & Hayes, E. R. (2000). *Handbook of Adult and Continuing Education* (New Ed.). Washington, DC.: American Association for Adult and Continuing Education.

CHAPTER 13

Perspective Transformation via Service-Learning in Family Life Education Methodology

Scott Tobias

13.1 Overview

Family Life Education Methodology is an upper-division course normally taken in the fall of one's senior year on the Stark Campus of Kent State University. The goals of the course include introducing and internalizing Family Life Education (FLE) as a professional identity, exploring how FLE can benefit communities through preventative programming, and allowing students to learn firsthand the process for establishing preventative programming for a community partner through the use of a modified service-learning project.

Service-learning has been shown to be beneficial to student learning in a variety of research findings (Astin & Sax, 1998; Eyler, Giles, Stenson, & Gray, 2001; Prentice, 2011; Tobias, 2013). Additionally, service-learning is identified as a high-impact practice by the Association of American Colleges and Universities (Kuh, 2008). In this course, service-learning requires students to engage as professionals-in-training with a community partner, reflect on service-learning experiences throughout the course of

S. Tobias (✉)
Human Development and Family Studies, Kent State University at Stark, North Canton, OH, USA

the class, and construct prevention-based programming based on current scientific research as a deliverable to the community partner at the end of the semester. The combination of these factors working in concert leads to deep learning via the service-learning component (Kuh, 2008). Embedded within a practitioner setting, this approach may foster a sense of perspective transformation from that of student to new professional (Tobias, 2013).

Mezirow's (1991) theory of adult learning centers on the concept of perspective transformation. Perspective transformation is situated in ten non-linear phases that a student may experience, though it is not necessary to experience all ten steps in order to successfully and completely transform one's perspective. A list of the ten phases of perspective transformation is presented in Table 13.1. Mezirow's theory argues learning is an ongoing process where students are asked to make meaning out of cognitively disorienting experiences they encounter. This disorientation is paired with new learning, facilitating a deeper and more nuanced understanding of the topic through the reorganization of held beliefs and perspectives. This process must be aided by opportunities for self-reflection throughout the duration of the learning experience. Bringle and Hatcher (1999b) note that reflection is necessary for student intellectual growth as well as aiding in synthesizing course material and research for application in a work environment.

Table 13.1 Mezirow's Phases of Transformation

1. A disorienting dilemma.
2. Self-examination with feelings of guilt or shame.
3. A critical assessment of epistemic, sociocultural, or psychic assumptions.
4. Recognition that one's discontent and the process of transformation are shared and that others have negotiated a similar change.
5. Exploration of options for new roles, relationships, and actions.
6. Planning of a course of action.
7. Acquisition of knowledge and skills for implementing one's plans.
8. Provisional trying of new roles.
9. Building of competence and self-confidence in new roles and relationships.
10. A reintegration into one's own life on the basis of conditions dictated by one's new perspective.
(Mezirow, 1991, p. 168)

13.2 Course Design

The FLE methodology course centers on utilizing the benefits of service-learning as viewed through the lens of perspective transformation. Specifically, the course asks students to construct five hours of detailed preventative programming for a community partner. This limited-scale project mirrors the process of constructing programming, much as they would if they were hired to create preventative programming as a professional. This programming follows the design model forwarded by Duncan and Goddard (2011) regarding the construction of preventative family programming. Much of the day-to-day work undertaken in class is put to immediate use aimed at utilizing new learning in productive ways in designing and constructing programming.

Initially, students are randomly assigned to a program "team" of 4–5 students who are tasked with identifying a topic that interests them as a group. Based on this discussion, they are then tasked with identifying a community agency which deals with their chosen topic. After making initial contact with the agency, the team must then design a brief needs assessment based on one or more interviews outside of class with a key informant at their chosen agency. The information collected during the interviews centers on agency background, needs, and potential self-identified areas of weakness in programmatic community offerings. Students compile the information from the interview(s) and, using qualitative data analysis skills previously learned in research methods courses, identify themes and areas of need that may be addressed through preventative programming by Family Life Educators.

Once an area of need is specifically identified by students, they are asked to begin constructing programming from the ground up, allowing them to experience all major aspects of programming construction. Typically this involves reading and compiling an annotated bibliography of at least 20 recent research articles relevant to the identified topic, establishing both general and specific change objectives which match agency needs with research findings, constructing moment-to-moment programming of at least five hours which builds toward stated learning goals and creating an assessment of participant learning for the programming. Students are provided weekly goals which establish a timeline for successfully completing their projects. The major weekly goals which do not vary include:

- Conduct a needs assessment of a student-chosen agency by the end of week three.
- Write a programming proposal including programming goal statement and rationale for the creation of programming utilizing the results of the needs assessment by the end of week five.
- Establish specific change objectives by the end of week seven.
- Creation of outcome measures based on change objectives by the end of week nine.
- Build lesson plans by identifying materials needed and utilizing research findings to inform plans by week 11.
- Revision of materials and completion of final project by the end of week 15.

The instructor, acting as a facilitator, sets weekly goals which match the needs of the class between the major goals listed above. The process is time intensive and asks students to simultaneously utilize what they are learning in class while activating existing knowledge gained in prior coursework to inform the choices being made.

Finished projects are professional in tone, appearance, and content. The program is expected to be comprehensive enough that it can be successfully executed by any member of the program construction team or by individuals at the community agency for which the programming was constructed. Additionally, the project is introduced to the community agency in a formal presentation at the end of the semester. During the final presentation, the entire process of program construction is reviewed for the community agency representative, decisions regarding programming choices are described, and links between programming and current research findings are outlined and explained. After the presentation, one copy of the finished project is delivered to the instructor for grading while another is given to the community agency representative.

13.3 HIGH-IMPACT PRACTICES

The FLE methodology course is one in which several elements of the high-impact practices identified by Kuh (2008) are utilized. Specifically, these high-impact practices include considerable time on meaningful tasks, faculty/student interactions on substantive matters, frequent performance feedback, activities that have applications on and off campus, and authentic connections made with peers, faculty and community partners. These practices are elaborated on in the following sections along with explanations of how the course facilitates their usage in relation to parallel aspects of perspective transformation.

13.3.1 Considerable Time Spent on Meaningful Tasks

In the FLE methodology course, students are asked to envision themselves as professionals in the field rather than students, leading to a more professionally situated approach to learning course content. Students are expected to read assigned text chapters and readings outside of course time and are also expected to be prepared to discuss in detail how these readings apply to their own programmatic construction. Much of class time is spent either in discussion regarding execution of learned content within each team or in active programming construction within teams; the instructor serves as a guide for any questions or concerns that arise.

The skills learned and utilized during class time are similar processes to a work environment. Students would need to undertake these same tasks in a collaborative professional setting to successfully construct preventative community programming. The process allows students to become more deeply engaged with the material and with the process of program construction, mirroring Mezirow's process of nuanced understanding and cognitive reorganization by pairing learning with new and challenging experiences. This meaningful work encourages the commencement of perspective transformation, with the end goal of students gaining a broader frame of reference and increased autonomy through the process of discourse (Mezirow, 1997).

13.3.2 Faculty and Students Interact on Substantive Matters

As students work to complete weekly goals during class time, class discussions are undertaken as they work in teams toward these goals. These discussions are an effort to allow students to explore the process of programming construction in an environment that allows for open questions and substantive feedback. This, in turn, informs both students and faculty regarding overall project progress as well as content mastery. Discussions may range from questions concerning abstract ideas and theory to more specific questions regarding discrete aspects of program construction. Since these students will soon find themselves in an independent work environment, these discussions allow for reflection on prior learning, the practical application of skills they have learned during prior coursework, and a Socratic Method of gaining information and refining one's own perspective and frame of reference. Perspective transformation identifies learning in such an environment, where the instructor acts as a facilitator, as focused on student learning, collaborative and hands-on (Mezirow, 1997).

13.3.3   Frequent Performance Feedback

While the Family Life Education Methodology course contains traditional exams as well as weekly goals which provide feedback to teams, the feedback must take on a more personalized approach given that students may be engaged in varying phases of perspective transformation. One of the most important methods to achieve this level of communication for both the faculty member as well as students is the frequent collection of, and individualized response to, guided journal entries and classroom discussions.

Reflexivity regarding one's own work is one of the cornerstones of service-learning (Bringle & Hatcher, 1999a) and perspective transformation (Mezirow, 1991). In the methodology course, students write ten guided journal entries over the course of a semester. This reflective process generally begins in week three after they have visited with and conducted a needs assessment of the community agency their team has chosen. Each guided journal entry is aligned with one of the ten phases of perspective transformation, beginning with phase one. The first prompt centers on preconceptions regarding the need for and availability of services prior to and after conducting the needs assessment at the selected community agency. Other prompt examples that have been utilized include, "What are some of the beliefs you hold regarding the population that the agency serves or about the agency itself? Where do these beliefs originate from?" (Phase 3), "Are there aspects of creating programming that have led to frustration to this point? How do you plan to overcome them as an individual? As a team?" (Phase 4), and "Describe your role as a professional on this project. Describe how it does or does not differ from your role as a student" (Phase 8). The instructor tailors these prompts to the needs of the class in an attempt to foster autonomy and critical reflexivity (Mezirow, 1997). Based on student feedback and discussions, the remaining nine prompts can be distributed where deemed most appropriate by the faculty member. Each response is read and responded to by the faculty member who can add insight or provide feedback regarding the students' response. This provides an opportunity for the students to contemplate faculty responses and encourages the successful completion of perspective transformation phases.

On a day-to-day basis, students engage in constructive dialogue about concepts they are learning in class, as well as how those concepts apply to their own experiences as they construct programming. While all teams are working on the same aspects of programming construction simultaneously, variations in how teams experience construction fosters lines of questioning that lead to fruitful and meaningful discussion about the process of programmatic construction. This process fosters autonomous thought, a key concept in transformative education (Mezirow, 1997). For example, groups working to incorporate current research findings into their programming may plan to utilize very different types of activities in their programs. While discussing the activities, the faculty member may pose questions which ask students to reflect on how these differing types of activities may be received by their respective target population(s) and the types of responses that may result. This leads to an iterative process of reflexivity and opportunities for feedback for students as they progress in constructing programming.

13.3.4 Activities That Have Applications to Settings On and Off Campus

Students must undertake a variety of activities in both on- and off-campus settings in order to successfully construct the necessary components of a complete program for a community partner. Researching existing community programming and resources on a chosen topic, conducting a needs assessment, identifying and interpreting recent scientific research, construction of programming activities appropriate for an identified client and the presentation of a finalized program to community professionals are examples of such activities. Given the need to utilize time and resources in productive ways to successfully complete the program construction, students must also master time management and skills associated with successfully working as a member of a group. Each of these skills is directly translatable to successfully working as a Family Life Educator in their own careers.

13.3.5 Authentic Connections Made with Peers, Faculty and Community

The nature of this course lends itself to meaningful and reflective discussions regarding the process of constructing preventative programming and working as a professional, rather than memorization of course content. It is necessary for students to interact in respectful and productive ways with peers in order to continually meet weekly (and semester-long) goals of completing program construction. In addition, students develop a sense of their own professional identity, shifting the interactions with faculty members from one of unequal power to peer-based interactions. The faculty member, as a guide, also learns about the students' progress in the role of a new professional. This insight allows for meaningful feedback throughout the course, as well as placing the faculty member as a resource for students when working with new learning moment to moment (Mezirow, 1997) and regarding professional issues.

Finally, students begin to establish networks of community contacts for whom they collaboratively construct programming. Since each team works with a different agency, students are exposed to a number of community resources dealing with a wide variety of topics. Interacting with these agencies allows students to learn a great deal about types of resources available to families in the community and begins to develop a sense of how various organizations work with each other to strengthen the community in general.

13.4 Summary

The Family Life Education Methodology course, utilizing service-learning, offers students the opportunity to operate as professionals by constructing preventative programming for a community partner. Under the guidance of a faculty member, they undertake the same process that a professional in the field would utilize in constructing programming. This process allows for multiple instances of high-impact practices identified by Kuh (2008) and, when paired with the theory of perspective transformation forwarded by Mezirow, provides an opportunity for students to problem-solve for the community while fostering a more fully developed sense of Family Life Education in practice and as future professionals.

Dr. Scott Tobias is an assistant professor of Human Development and Family Studies at Kent State University at Stark in North Canton, Ohio.

References

Astin, A. W., & Sax, L. J. (1998). How undergraduates are affected by service participation. *Journal of College Student Development, 39*, 251–263.

Bringle, R. G., & Hatcher, J. A. (1999a). Implementing service-learning in higher education. *Journal of Higher Education, 67*(2), 221–239.

Bringle, R. G., & Hatcher, J. A. (1999b). Reflection in service learning: Making meaning of experience. *Educational Horizons, 77*(4), 179–185.

Duncan, S. F., & Goddard, H. W. (2011). *Family life education: Principles and practices for effective outreach*. Thousand Oaks, CA: Sage.

Eyler, J., Giles, D. E., Stenson, C. M., & Gray, C. J. (2001). At a glance: What we know about the effects of service-learning on college students, faculty, institutions, and communities, 1993–2000. Retrieved May 25, 2013 from Campus Compact Website http://www.compact.org/resources/downloads/aag.pdf

Kuh, G. (2008). *High-impact educational practices: What they are, who has access to them, and why they matter*. Washington, DC: The Association of American Colleges & Universities.

Mezirow, J. (1991). *Transformative dimensions of adult learning*. San Francisco, CA: Jossey-Bass.

Mezirow, J. (1997). Transformative learning: Theory to practice. *New Directions for Adult and Continuing Education, 74*, 5–12.

Prentice, M. (2011). Civic engagement among community college students through service learning. *Community College Journal of Research and Practice, 35*(11), 842–854.

Tobias, S. (2013). Perspective transformation through service-learning: Student reflections. *AURCO Journal*, 209–220.

CHAPTER 14

Reverse Planning a Service Learning Activity for an Undergraduate Public Policy Course

Jacki Fitzpatrick

14.1 Reverse Planning Principles

Reverse engineering is the process of analyzing systems to identify the (1) systems' key components and (2) relationships between the components. This engineering process relies upon knowledge of the finality of a system (e.g., finished version of a product, outcome of an event). After the finality is known, it is deconstructed to learn more about the system and plan for adaptations/improvements in the future (Syrowik, 2003). Deconstruction makes it possible to extrapolate (from a specific system) information that is relevant to other systems/issues. This process has been used in fields such as computer science (Burd & Munro, 2000) and manufacturing (Sokovic & Kopac, 2006). Reverse engineering or planning principles have been used to develop educational software (Choquet & Corbière, 2006), but have not been commonly applied to educational content (e.g., course assignments).

Instructors can use reverse planning (RP) principles to develop course assignments/activities. More specifically, teachers can conceptualize their intended endpoints (e.g., "To what experiences/events will students have been exposed? How will the exposure be linked to course concepts?").

J. Fitzpatrick (✉)
Human Development and Family Studies, Texas Tech University,
Lubbock, TX, USA

After instructors have envisioned these endpoints, they can design the learning activities. Specific elements of the activities (e.g., location, tasks) are chosen based on their degree of alignment with the endpoints (e.g., Korey, 2010). This approach can increase the likelihood that teachers are creating relevant and useful activities for students.

RP principles might be particularly helpful to instructors who use field-based experiences (FBEs). FBEs can give students exposure to events/processes that would be unmanageable in the traditional classroom (e.g., Eckerman Pitton, 2006; Wong, 2007). In addition, FBEs allow students to learn from community members (e.g., clients, service providers) who have experiential knowledge of social/familial conditions (Baum, 1997; Jarrott, 2001; Murray, Lampinen, & Kelley-Soderholm, 2006). Indeed, as some clients have lived with challenges for years, the clients might be more knowledgeable than students/teachers about such conditions (e.g., Cohen, Hatchett, & Eastridge, 2006). FBEs such as service learning (SL) can have significant risks, so these activities require planning and supervision (Butin, 2006). RP can be one approach to the planning process. I will describe how I used RP to create an SL activity.

14.2 ACTIVITIES HAVE APPLICATIONS TO DIFFERENT SETTINGS ON/OFF CAMPUS

The SL activity was designed for an undergraduate public policy course. The course addresses how broad social policies (e.g., health care, employment) can impact families. A review of policies is necessary, but somewhat abstract and does not necessarily facilitate students' engagement in policies.

It is important for students to be able to see the linkages between policy and service issues in the real world (Crutsinger, Pookulangara, Tran, & Duncan, 2004). I was concerned that traditional course components (e.g., lecture, group discussion) would be insufficient to build the linkages. So, I utilized RP principles to envision how I wanted to facilitate the links. By the end of the course, I wanted students to have had (1) meaningful interactions with community members (e.g., clients, staff members), (2) on-site agency involvement in which members were dealing with policy issues, (3) opportunities to contribute to the daily functioning of the agency, and (4) opportunities to delineate the links that they identified. However, I had to balance this vision within some course limitations. For example, this was a night course and I knew (from prior semesters) that many students can't engage in FBEs during daytime hours. In addition, there were time constraints from other course assignments that students would have to complete. So, I needed an FBE that had the potential for high policy exposure in a limited number of night/weekend hours. Thus, I decided that SL would be the best FBE fit.

14.3 Students Experience Diversity Through Contact with People Who Are Different from Themselves

SL gives students exposure to events that are beyond the traditional classroom, and sometimes beyond students' life experiences (e.g., Cohen et al., 2006). Of course, it is possible that some students' families have experienced situations (e.g., disabilities, poverty) in which policies impacted them. Such students have their own insights into policy/service issues. However, this type of exposure is not guaranteed for the whole class. In addition, there is no desire for all students to have life crises that mandate such exposure. Thus, SL can be a way to provide a consistent experience for multiple students in the same course. In contrast to an internship, SL students typically (1) work fewer hours and (2) have less developed professional skills (e.g., intake, assessment). Despite these limitations, SL students can gain knowledge and contribute to community agencies in a relatively brief time (e.g., Fitzpatrick, 2013a; Murray et al., 2006). SL facilitates the linkages between course concepts and actual social systems (Ballard & Elmore, 2009). This linkage can be particularly helpful when instructors are teaching abstract concepts (e.g., Eyler, 2002), such as public policy.

Next, I had to choose a community agency (at which students would complete SL work). It might have been possible to select an agency that focused on policy creation (e.g., city administration, school board, advocacy group). However, such a selection might have kept students' policy exposure at an abstract level. Instead, I wanted students to see community members working within the service system (which is dictated by policies). I also wanted students to see members who were dealing with multiple policy issues. So, I chose the local chapter of Ronald McDonald House Charities (RMHC).

RMHC provides housing for family members when children are receiving medical care at nearby facilities (e.g., hospitals). Families can be referred by medical staff (Desai, Ng, & Bryant, 2002) or make direct requests for housing. Although some families might have advance notice that medical care (and housing) will be needed, many families deal with immediate child crises, such as consumption of poisonous substances (e.g., Cherry, Lowry, Velez, Cotrell, & Keyes, 2002) or car accidents. Thus, these families are often unfamiliar with the policy challenges that they will face. In addition to health care, many families need to address employment, education (for siblings) and economic issues quickly (e.g., Miedema, Easley, Fortin, Hamilton, & Mathews, 2008). RMHC staff members assist families to address policy/service issues (1) throughout their time at the house and (2) in the transition to other locations (e.g., rehabilitation centers, families' home communities). Indeed, RMHC care can contribute to children's well-being after families have left the housing facilities (e.g., Dockett, 2004).

Due to space limitations, families that live in this city are not permitted to stay in the local RMHC house. Rooms are available for families from other communities/states. RMHC staff reported that their clients come from multiple states and continents (e.g., South America, Europe). Thus, this local agency would give students an opportunity to meet a diverse clientele.

14.4 STUDENTS SPEND CONSIDERABLE AMOUNTS OF TIME ON MEANINGFUL TASKS

Students were required to complete 15 SL hours, but were limited to a maximum of three hours per week. I did not want students to complete all hours in a marathon session (e.g., Spring Break) because students might be (1) more focused on fulfilling hours than learning, (2) less likely to make authentic connections and (3) have no opportunity for reflection between events. In addition, my schedule requirement increased the likelihood that students would observe a broader range of clients. Although a few families might stay at the house for several months, most stay for briefer periods. Thus, students would likely interact with more clients if students were required to engage in SL over multiple weeks.

The SL activity was based on a partnership model rather than a project model. In a project model, students work on a singular task, product, or system for a community agency (Flinders, Nicholson, Carlascio, & Gilb, 2012). This model might work in environments in which there is a highly stable routine. However, I did not think that this model would fit RMHC. Their client families face multiple issues on a daily basis, and the families' well-being is often directly tied to their children's health. As health status can change dramatically, the families' situations are tenuous. Thus, RMHC staff spends much time responding to families' needs of a particular day. In this context, it made more sense to use a partnership model (Flinders et al., 2012), in which students were expected to adapt to the partner's (RMHC) task demands. Each time that students entered the house, they were advised by an RMHC mentor (e.g., staff member, volunteer coordinator) of (1) salient events that would impact the shift and (2) tasks that the students should complete. In addition to assigned tasks, students were encouraged to identify other ways in which they might be helpful. This approach to SL tasks (1) respected the dynamics of RMHC, (2) increased the likelihood that students would perform meaningful tasks, and (3) gave students exposure to realistic agency conditions. Indeed, the RMHC staff could determine which tasks would be most meaningful for each student during each three-hour shift. The RMHC dynamics were explained to students before beginning SL work (Fitzpatrick, 2013b). It was hoped that this information would facilitate (1) student responsiveness and (2) more authentic connections.

14.5 Students Receive Frequent Performance Feedback

Students received feedback from the instructor via their written papers. Students also received feedback via non-graded discussions with the instructor and RMHC staff. SL requires that students spend time outside of class and with community members (Timmermans & Bouman, 2005). Although this arrangement can be advantageous for students, it meant that I would not be on-site and observing them (during SL shifts). Thus, it was necessary to develop a means for (1) students to share information about their insights and (2) me to give students feedback about their performance. Rather than complete a single summary paper, I decided that students would complete five brief papers. Each paper would be in response to a single SL shift. This multi-paper approach aligned with the immediacy of SL events (Cashman & Seifer, 2008).

The approach also seemed to fit the nature of RMHC's clientele. Given that multiple families might enter/leave the house in a single semester, students were likely to know some clients briefly. If students only completed a single summary paper, they might lose recall of particular families/events and simply create an amalgam of their experience. Instead, I wanted students to evaluate the situational impact of policies (e.g., Medicaid made a difference for a certain family).

The papers were not simply a journaling activity in which students reported thoughts/emotions (e.g., "public policy is boring"). Rather, the papers required that students make links between course concepts and the RMHC environment. Students had to respond to questions such as "How do disability policies facilitate or hinder the families' experiences?". This question format is consistent with recommendations for academically based SL (Eyler, 2002; Timmermans & Bouman, 2005).

For each paper assignment, students were given two question options. Students had to select one question (to which they responded in the paper). This process gave students flexibility (e.g., Mio & Barker-Hackett, 2003), as it allowed them to select the question that was most relevant to a shift. The choice empowered students to exercise some decision-making initiative, which is consistent with SL and academic principles (Farren, 2010; Roschelle, Turpin, & Elias, 2000).

In addition to papers, students were given opportunities to debrief their experiences with me and/or RMHC staff. The debriefing process allows individuals to discuss their reactions (e.g., fears, frustrations) to educational experiences (Swan et al., 2007). As students witnessed some difficult events at RMHC (e.g., parents informed of children's diagnoses), the debriefing let them discuss such events in a non-graded context. This process created opportunities for meaningful interactions between me and the students.

14.6 Suggestions for Future FBEs

Based on this SL teaching experience, I offer a few suggestions. I recognize that the suggestions might not be a good fit for all family studies programs, courses, or FBEs. I simply list suggestions as a potential resource.

First, engage in some planning approach for each FBE. If the RP approach does not seem to be a good fit, try other approaches. When possible, include community members in the planning process (Fitzpatrick, 2013b). A well-planned activity conveys that teachers take their responsibilities seriously. A poorly planned FBE demonstrates some disrespect for students/community members, and could do more harm than good (e.g., Butin, 2006). It is understood that instructors cannot foresee every problem or contingency. However, they can make a good faith effort to plan effectively.

Second, consider how each FBE fits the course content. The FBE gives students exposure to off-campus environments, but exposure alone is not sufficient. Rather, each FBE should foster students' knowledge of particular course concepts (e.g., Ballard & Elmore, 2009). If students are utilizing community resources, then the community should also benefit from the students' presence (Eckerman Pitton, 2006). Thus, an FBE should be a value-added experience.

Third, be mindful that an FBE requires persistent monitoring. It is not appropriate for instructors to consider an FBE as someone else's issue (e.g., "Once the students go into agencies, the students are not my problem"). Rather, teachers should be as engaged in FBE as any other course responsibility (e.g., writing lectures, creating exams). Indeed, Eby (2001) indicated that instructors should hold equally high standards for FBEs and research. Teachers who meet such standards will create an FBE that benefits students and community members.

References

Ballard, S., & Elmore, B. (2009). A labor of love: Constructing a service-learning syllabus. *The Journal of Effective Teaching, 9*, 70–76.

Baum, H. (1997). Social science, social work and surgery: Teaching what students need to practice planning. *Journal of the American Planning Association, 63*, 179–188.

Burd, E., & Munro, M. (2000). Using evolution to evaluate reverse engineering technologies: Mapping the process of software change. *Journal of Systems and Software, 53*, 43–51.

Butin, D. (2006). The limits of service-learning in higher education. *The Review of Higher Education, 29*, 473–498.

Cashman, S., & Seifer, S. (2008). Service learning: An integral part of undergraduate public health. *American Journal of Preventive Medicine, 35*, 273–278.

Cherry, D., Lowry, L., Velez, L., Cotrell, C., & Keyes, D. (2002). Elemental mercury poisoning in a family of seven. *Family and Community Health, 24*, 1–8.

Choquet, C., & Corbière, A. (2006). Reengineering framework for systems in education. *Educational Technology & Society, 9*, 228–241.

Cohen, H., Hatchett, B., & Eastridge, D. (2006). Intergenerational service-learning: An innovative teaching strategy to infuse gerontology content into foundation courses. *Journal of Gerontological Social Work, 48*, 161–178.

Crutsinger, C., Pookulangara, S., Tran, G., & Duncan, K. (2004). Collaborative service learning: A winning proposition for industry and education. *Journal of Family and Consumer Sciences, 96*, 46–52.

Desai, P., Ng, J., & Bryant, S. (2002). Care of children and families in the CICU: A focus on their developmental, psychosocial and spiritual needs. *Critical Care Nursing Quarterly, 25*, 88–97.

Dockett, S. (2004). "Everyone was really happy to see me!': The importance of friendships in the return to school of children with chronic illness. *Australian Journal of Early Childhood, 29,* 27–32.

Eby, J. (2001). The promise of service-learning for family science: An overview. *Journal of Teaching in Marriage and Family, 1*(3), 1–13.

Eckerman Pitton, D. (2006). Bullying: A middle school service-learning project. *Action in Teacher Education, 28,* 29–41.

Eyler, J. (2002). Reflection: Linking service and learning—Linking students and communities. *Journal of Social Issues, 58,* 517–534.

Farren, A. (2010). An educational strategy for teaching standardized nursing languages. *International Journal of Nursing Terminologies and Classifications, 21,* 3–13.

Fitzpatrick, J. (2013a). The application of Kram's mentorship functions to a service learning assignment. *Journal of College and Character, 14,* 185–192.

Fitzpatrick, J. (2013b). A service learning assignment in an undergraduate public policy course. *Journal of Regional Engagement, 2,* 85–96.

Flinders, B., Nicholson, L., Carlascio, A., & Gilb, K. (2012). The partnership model for service-learning programs: A step-by-step approach. *American Journal of Health Sciences, 4,* 67–77.

Jarrott, S. (2001). Service-learning at dementia care programs: A social history project. *Journal of Teaching in Marriage and Family, 1*(4), 1–12.

Korey, J. (2010). MAC3 evaluation: Monitoring process, documenting outcomes. *MathAMATYC Educator, 1,* 62–68.

Miedema, B., Easley, J., Fortin, P., Hamilton, R., & Mathews, M. (2008). The economic impact on families when a child is diagnosed with cancer. *Current Oncology, 15,* 173–178.

Mio, J., & Barker-Hackett, L. (2003). Reaction papers and journal writing as techniques for assessing resistance in multicultural courses. *Journal of Multicultural Counseling & Development, 31,* 12–19.

Murray, C., Lampinen, A., & Kelley-Soderholm, E. (2006). Teaching family systems theory through service-learning. *Counselor Education & Supervision, 46,* 44–58.

Roschelle, A., Turpin, J., & Elias, R. (2000). Who learns from service learning? *American Behavioral Scientist, 43,* 839–847.

Sokovic, M., & Kopac, J. (2006). Re(reverse engineering) as necessary phase by rapid product development. *Journal of Materials Processing Technology, 175,* 398–403.

Swan, K., Mazur, J., Trullinger, L., Brock, D., Ross, A., Holman, A., & Yost, J. (2007). The voice of reason: Social studies pre-service teachers debrief their initial experiences with technology integration. *Social Studies Research and Practice, 2,* 261–279.

Syrowik, D. (2003). Restriking the balance: The Uniform Computer Information Transactions Act (UCITA) and reverse engineering. *Michigan Bar Journal, 82*, 30–34.

Timmermans, S., & Bouman, J. (2005). Seven ways of teaching and learning: University-community partnerships at baccalaureate institutions. *Journal of Community Practice, 12*, 89–101.

Wong, P. (2007). Six multicultural service-learning lessons I learned in the wake of Hurricane Katrina. *Multicultural Education, 15*, 52–54.

CHAPTER 15

Service-Learning Design Through a Management Model

Kendra Brandes, G. Kevin Randall, and Lauren Leach-Steffens

Service-learning has been identified as one of nine high-impact educational practices recommended for effective course design (Kuh, 2008). Learning by doing, the basis of John Dewey's educational models of the late 1800s, firmly established this as a best practice in the early years of modern American education (Dewey, 1917). Models incorporating experiential learning are found on a wide benefit spectrum ranging from student volunteering, with most of the benefit going to the recipient of the services, to student internships where the student is the primary recipient of the *learning through doing* model. However, current definitions of service-learning focus upon the integration of multiple components.

K. Brandes (✉)
Department of Family and Consumer Sciences, Bradley University, Peoria, IL, USA

G.K. Randall
Department of Family and Consumer Sciences, Sam Houston State University, Huntsville, TX, USA

L. Leach-Steffens
School of Health Science and Wellness, Northwest Missouri State University, Maryville, MO, USA

Table 15.1 Six Attributes of Effective High-Impact Programs

1. Students spend considerable amounts of time on meaningful tasks.
2. Faculty and student peers interact about substantive matters.
3. Students experience diversity through contact with people who are different than themselves.
4. Students receive frequent performance feedback.
5. Activities have applications to different settings on/off campus.
6. Authentic connections are made with peers, faculty, community, and/or the university.

Kuh (2008)

As defined by the National Service-Learning Clearing House (n.d.), "Service-learning is a teaching and learning strategy that integrates meaningful community service with instruction and reflection to enrich the learning experience, teach civic responsibility, and strengthen communities." When the content to be learned is a specific skill, the learning component of a service-learning activity is easily defined. For example, students studying construction management gain valuable knowledge when they engage in house construction through service with a Habitat for Humanity project. However, many learning outcomes and activities related to the human sciences are not so specific. Thus, developing specific learning outcomes and guidelines for activities to accomplish those outcomes is essential. This chapter describes a service-learning project created within the framework of two models: (1) Fink's (2003) taxonomy of significant learning and (2) Goldsmith's (2010) resource management model. Together these models provided structure for designing service-learning activities that incorporate many of the attributes of high-impact practices recognized as standards for effective teaching and course design (Kuh, 2008; Table 15.1).

15.1 Theoretical Underpinnings of Service-Learning

Any discussion of learning taxonomies should include Bloom's Taxonomy of Learning (1956), a well-known, frequently used scaffold for learning activities and course design. Bloom's hierarchy of learning tasks begins with acquiring fundamental knowledge and progresses through thinking that becomes increasingly analytical. Although Bloom's Taxonomy contains affective components, the cognitive components are most well

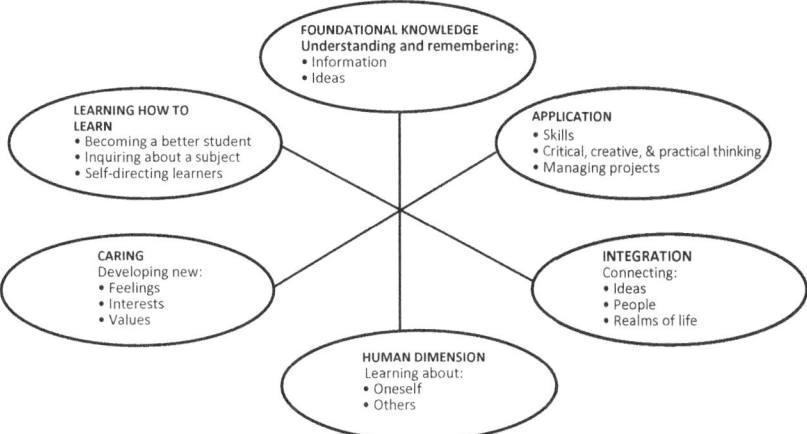

Fig. 15.1 Taxonomy of significant learning. Adapted from *Creating significant learning experiences: An integrated approach to designing college courses*, by L.D. Fink, 2003, p. 30. Copyright 2013 by Jossey-Bass, San Francisco, CA

known and widely used. A recent taxonomy developed by Fink (2003) places more emphasis on areas related to cognitive and affective changes within the learner (Fig. 15.1). Fink's overlapping dimensions of learning go beyond mastery of content. He describes the process of course design and teaching using an integrated approach. As opposed to a linear, subject-centered approach where courses are designed around topics to be covered, he proposes course design based upon learning outcomes. Beginning with the desired outcomes for student learning and working backward through learning activities, he arrives at the topics to be covered—the foundational knowledge. The dimensions of significant learning are not hierarchal, but rather are integrated, resulting in a structure ideally suited for service-learning projects.

Bringle and Hatcher (1999) include the processes of structure, feedback, and values clarification as necessary components for a positive learning experience. Goldsmith (2010) utilizes these processes and others in a resource management model that allows students to identify, design, and implement a project that is specific to their own areas of interest. Goldsmith's management model is an ideal complement to Fink's suggestions for course or project design.

15.2 THE SERVICE-LEARNING PROJECT

This service-learning experience was incorporated into a core course within a Family and Consumer Sciences (FCS) program in a private, medium-sized university. The course content, Family Systems and Resource Management, is a component of a curriculum core that spans all majors within the FCS department including Community Wellness, Dietetics, Education, General Family and Consumer Sciences, Hospitality Leadership, and Retail Merchandising. Students tend to view each major as a separate field of study, unrelated to one another or to the overall field of FCS. On evaluations, students commented that they failed to see the relevance of the management process to their own field of study. The service-learning project was added to the course to create the opportunity for students from different majors to work together and to apply steps from a management model to a "real life" project in cooperation with a community agency. After the first year, it became evident that the project taught the students more than course content. Other significant learning appeared to be taking place (Brandes & Randall, 2011).

The structure of the service-learning project was adapted from a model developed by Leach-Steffens (2005). A management model (Fig. 15.2) by Goldsmith (2010) provided the framework for integrating service-learning with course content. The class was divided into randomly assigned groups of three or four students. Each group was responsible for locating a community agency willing to work with the students to meet a need or goal as identified by the agency. This format is consistent with the project-based service-learning model which is the most favorable use of community agency time and resources when students are engaged in a project of short (semester long) duration (Tyron et al., 2008). "Many organizations have special projects that they lack the capacity to do. Having students with specific skills do those projects can fill those capacity gaps"

1. Identify Problem, Need, or Goal
2. Clarify Values
3. Identify Resources
4. Decide, Plan, & Implement
5. Accomplish Goals & Evaluate

Feedback

Fig. 15.2 The resource management model. Adapted from *Resource management for individuals and families*, by E.B. Goldsmith, 2010, p. 6. Copyright 2010 by Prentice Hall

(Tyron et al., 2008, p. 22). Students were provided with contact information for local agencies, but were given the freedom to contact groups not included in the list. The instructor provided guidance when it was requested, but allowed students to generate ideas based upon their own experiences. In doing so, the list of possible community sites is longer and more varied than a list provided by the instructor and increases the likelihood of a match between student interests and the nature of the service activity. Students were given guidelines (Leach-Steffens, 2005) designed to insure that each project aligned with each step of the management model. Because the first step of the management model is to work with an agency or group to identify a need, students were not allowed to join a service activity already in progress. The project had to be original and based upon the needs of the community agency. The project had to be planned, completed, and evaluated within the semester. Each student was required to contribute a minimum of 20 hours to the project.

15.3 Designing Backwards

The learning outcomes of the project described in this chapter included two components. The first was an understanding of the steps of a resource management model (see Fig. 15.2). Traditional college-aged students often think of resources in terms of money or material goods, but their own time and talents tend to be overlooked. The act of planning resource use through a defined sequence of steps is a concept new to many students. A second learning outcome was increased appreciation for the relationship between students' specific area of study and civic responsibility. Each of Fink's categories of significant learning was relevant to the learning outcomes intended for this course.

While the management model was part of the course content of this class, it is adaptable to almost any subject and allows the course design process to "work backwards" by designing course activities based upon learning outcomes rather than on specific content. Additionally, the value of this model allows the students to design course activities based upon their specific disciplines or areas of interest. For example, dietetics students may design a project that links nutritional information with community agencies that require such expertise. Students studying child development may create a project based upon their own areas of interest. Ideally, students from different areas of study will form a group that creates a transdisciplinary approach to a community agency need or goal. Whatever the makeup of the group, the value derives from turning much of the planning of the learning activities over to the students. Morton (1995) identified different service paradigms and proposed that student outcomes reflect the degree to which students perceive being well matched with a type of service-learning project they find interesting or meaningful.

15.4 Attributes of Effective High-Impact Programs

Table 15.2 provides one example of a service-learning project conducted using the steps in the management process. The table also reveals the relationship of each step to high-impact practices and to Fink's dimensions of significant learning. The project, referred to as the Butterfly Project, simply began to replant a butterfly garden at an assisted living center for developmentally disabled adults. We highlight this project because many of the high-impact practices were readily apparent as the students worked through the project.

15.5 Students Spend Considerable Amounts of Time on Meaningful Tasks

Using this model, each student group plans, conducts, and evaluates a project over one semester. While a single semester often seems too short a time, experiencing the complete cycle from goal or need identification to project evaluation facilitates students' understanding of the process. Allowing students to work with community agencies to identify agency specific needs or goals fosters higher order thinking as students must evaluate and analyze values and resources of both students and the agency. Duration of at least a semester helps establish relationships between students and the community groups they choose to serve.

15.6 Faculty and Students Interact About Substantive Matters

Groups meet with the selected agency to identify the need or goal, and then meet with faculty to discuss and approve the project. Groups must present the initial idea to the class as a whole and respond to questions and

Table 15.2 Service-Learning Design Through a Management Model

Steps in the management process	Example project: The Butterfly Garden	High-impact practices	Fink's dimensions of significant learning
Step One: Identify a problem, need, or goal	Residents of an assisted living center needed a butterfly garden replanted. Students agreed to design and replant the garden	Activities have applications to different settings on/off the campus	Application: students engage in creative and practical thinking
Feedback	Student group meets with instructor to discuss project in relation to class requirements	Students receive frequent performance feedback	Foundational Knowledge: students review and apply the management steps to their project
Step Two: Clarify values	Students met with center director and learned that his first priority was to provide his residents with social opportunities—both with each other and with members of the community at large (the students)	Students experience diversity through contact with people different than themselves	Human Dimension: learning about oneself and others
Step Three: Identify resources	Center will provide tools and funding for plants Students will provide time, labor, and opportunities for residents to help	Students spend considerable amounts of time on meaningful tasks	Learning how to learn: self-directed learning Butterfly garden design is not is the class text. Students must structure their own learning
Feedback	Student groups present a detailed project plan to the class, answer questions and respond to feedback from their classmates	Faculty and student peers interact about substantial matters	Application: critical and practical thinking
Step Four: Decide, plan, and implement	Students meet with residents, research and order plants, and begin to prepare garden bed	Students spend considerable amounts of time on meaningful tasks	Application

(*continued*)

Table 15.2 (continued)

Steps in the management process	Example project: The Butterfly Garden	High-impact practices	Fink's dimensions of significant learning
Feedback: Return to Step Three	Students learn that the director would like to enlarge the garden and build a sidewalk. Initially they do not question, but after working with pick axes and shovels on semi-frozen ground they realize they do not have the physical resources to complete the project Instructor suggests they return to Step Three and reevaluate resources	Students receive frequent performance feedback	Application: managing projects Human Dimension: learning about oneself
Step Five: Accomplish goals and evaluate	• Garden and sidewalk are completed • Residents, one by one, join the project • Students use their own money to purchase butterfly larvae kits for residents	Authentic connections are made with peers and the community	Human Dimension: learning about self and others Caring: verbal and written evaluation suggests a strong sense of civic responsibility Fundamental Knowledge: students gain experience with the management process
Evaluation and Feedback	Students present project to class and receive verbal and written feedback from their peers and instructor	Faculty and student peers interact about substantial matters	Integration: connecting ideas, people, and realms of life

comments. This presentation—question and answer format occurs several times during the semester to maintain feedback at all steps of the management process.

Students are given a great deal of freedom to work alongside a community agency, identifying a need and planning the project. Students, engaged in projects of their own design, are more likely to achieve learning outcomes that lead to changes within themselves. For example, Fink's (2003) dimension of *caring* cannot evolve from the pages of a textbook. In the Butterfly Project, it was an unexpected outcome that developed as students watched developmentally disabled adults overcome their challenges (often in the form of social interaction abilities) and join the work on the project. The project length—one semester—was enough time for authentic relationships between students and center residents to develop.

15.7 Students Experience Diversity Through Contact with People Who Are Different Than Themselves

Many, if not most, service-learning projects take place within the community and offer ample opportunity for interaction with people from all walks of life. Once students step out of the campus comfort zone and interact with members of the community, they must adapt to the characteristics of the agency members they have chosen to serve. Students may encounter lifestyles and value systems different from their own. When planning the project using the manage model, students are led through a process requiring them to examine goals and values early in the project. For example, the goal identified for the Butterfly Project was the redesign and replanting of a small butterfly garden. An important value identified by the center was the opportunity for social interaction for center residents by encouraging them to work with the students. This seemingly simple project engaged a group of young college women with developmentally disabled adults, hard physical labor, feelings of being overwhelmed, and ultimately, feelings of success and of close relationship to the residents of the assisted living center. Team members described their feelings about the project during the final presentation to the class. When digging in the frozen ground, the project felt impossible. They admitted to being close to tears and seriously thinking of dropping the class because this was not what they had "signed up" for. Once they began working with the residents (planting and creating the garden), none of those cold, difficult days mattered. They (the residents) were so happy and excited. The students stated that the project went beyond anything they imagined it could be.

15.8 STUDENTS RECEIVE FREQUENT PERFORMANCE FEEDBACK

Feedback, built into the management model, facilitates continual discussion of project goals and processes both with peers and faculty. This is especially important during the planning stages of the project when student groups must articulate goals and the steps to achieve them. Feedback may occur at any time during the project and provides a structure for objectively examining setbacks and problems that can so easily occur in any service-learning project. Feedback occurs formally as part of the course structure at the beginning of the semester, when students gain approval for the plan from the instructor, and at midterm when the teams present the plan to the entire class. Informal feedback occurs much more frequently as teams are encouraged to "check in" regarding their progress. Structure for checking in may vary with the size and makeup of the class, but the instructor should meet with each group at least every other week to be sure that activities are progressing according to plans. This also allows the instructor to determine how well the group is functioning as a unit.

Some students sail through the process with little or no project adjustment. The value of feedback in the management process becomes apparent when problems occur. Placing the structure of a service-learning project within the context of a process removes some of the negative feelings that can occur when planned activities collapse. In the Butterfly Garden example, students felt that the project had failed at a midpoint because the center requested a much larger garden and the addition of a sidewalk. The project suddenly seemed beyond their ability. They felt that "complaining" about the change in plans was inappropriate. Feedback became a necessary step at this point. When encouraged to meet with the center director to "reevaluate resources" (Table 15.2, Step Three), the process became manageable. The students learned that the director never intended for them to complete all of the activities on their own. Discussion was more comfortable when it focused on processes rather than on the students themselves.

15.9 SUMMARY

A project designed through a management model has the potential to include many attributes of effective high-impact practices. The management model allows course design to "work backwards" to develop learning activities based upon learning outcomes, arriving, finally, at the foundational knowledge, or, the topics most necessary to cover. This project is applicable to almost any topic and may be adapted to resource management needs beyond the classroom.

REFERENCES

Bloom, B. S. (Ed.). (1956). *Taxonomy of educational objectives. The classification of educational goals. Handbook I: Cognitive domain.* New York: McKay.

Brandes, K., & Randall, G. K. (2011). Service learning and civic responsibility: Assessing aggregate and individual level change. *International Journal of Teaching and Learning in Higher Education, 23*(1), 20–29.

Bringle, R. C., & Hatcher, J. A. (1999). Reflection in service learning: Making meaning of experience. *Educational Horizons, 77*, 179–185.

Dewey, J. (1917). *Democracy and education.* New York: Macmillan.

Fink, L. D. (2003). *Creating significant learning experiences: An integrated approach to designing college courses.* San Francisco, CA: Jossey-Bass.

Goldsmith, E. B. (2010). *Resource management for individuals and families* (4th ed.). Saddle River, NJ: Prentice Hall.

Kuh, G. (2008). *High-impact educational practices: What they are, who has access to them, and why they matter.* Washington, DC: AAC&U.

Leach-Steffens, L. (2005). *FCS 424, Management Project Booklet.* Unpublished class materials, Department of Family and Consumer Sciences, Northwest State University, Maryville, Missouri.

Morton, K. (1995). The irony of service: Charity, project, and social change in service-learning. *Michigan Journal of Community Service Learning, 2*, 19–32.

National Service-Learning Clearing House. (n.d.). What is service-learning? Retrieved May 28, 2013 from http://www.servicelearning.org/what-is-service-learning

Tyron, E., Stoecker, R., Martin, A., Seblonka, K., Hilgendorf, A., & Nellis, N. (2008, Spring). The challenge of short-term service-learning. *Michigan Journal of Community Service-Learning, 14*(2), 16–26.

CHAPTER 16

Service Learning in Family Life Education: Incorporating High-Impact Strategies in Undergraduate Family Science Programming

Anita Glee Bertram and Brandon Burr

16.1 SERVICE LEARNING

Service-learning in the context of Family Life Education academic programming is identified as an effective way to help students understand concepts that they have learned through their Family Life Education texts and classroom activities through applied, often field-based, experiences (Hamon, 2002; Knapp & Stubblefield, 2000). The focus of the service-learning process is unique from experiential learning (more benefitting the student) and volunteerism (more benefitting the recipient(s) of the volunteer efforts), in that the intention is to benefit both the student and the recipient(s) of the service activity, both of which positively contribute to the community (Deeley, 2010). Additionally, service-learning activities offer a unique opportunity for student growth through allowing students to make connections between conceptual classroom information and experiences gained through field/site-based activities.

A.G. Bertram (✉) • B. Burr
Human Environmental Sciences, University of Central Oklahoma, Edmond, OK, USA

Some academic programs may over-emphasize the development of skills and strategies in Family Life Education, limiting focus on conceptual and theoretical foundations which can enhance family professionals' ability to innovatively develop new strategies and adapt to different situations (Darling, Fleming, & Cassidy, 2009). Thus, carefully planned service-learning experiences provide opportunities for students to integrate newfound classroom knowledge and theoretical concepts into community service, which also acts as a solid training ground for students to become more engaged citizens. Best practices in Family Life Education underscore the need for the educator to "know the audience" with which they are working and serving (e.g. Duncan & Goddard, 2011). Service-learning can provide a valuable opportunity to learn about the population with which students will serve and work.

Applied experiences in family science/studies programs in terms of field experiences, practicums, internships, service-learning opportunities, etc. have grown substantially over the past 50 years (Smart & Berke, 2004). Many applied components to family science undergraduate programs are utilized as valuable career preparation. Thus, applied field-based experiences such as academic internships afford students opportunities to develop professional skills to more effectively compete for family service positions in the job market. Smart and Berke (2004) suggest that out-of-class learning experiences prior to entering the academic internship enable students to begin connecting classroom knowledge and concepts in applied settings and acquire professional skills in order to be better prepared and more fully benefit from the internship experience. Thus, service-learning course opportunities may allow students to begin to fine-tune knowledge and skill sets to later become better prepared interns and family professionals. These learning opportunities may be available through a number of different avenues. Because "family life education is relevant across the life span, is inclusive of all types of families, and is designed to meet the true needs of the target audience" (Ballard & Taylor, 2012, p. 1) regardless of the focus major of the student, service-learning venues and opportunities abound in society and potentially represent numerous, rich opportunities for students to connect classroom and applied experiences, gain professional skills and prepare for professional work, grow personally, and make positive contributions to the community.

At the instructional level, the success of the service-learning experience and the learning environment often takes careful planning and focus. If students are unable to make a clear connection between the classroom-learning component and the service activity, confusion and frustration are likely to occur (Deeley, 2010; Hamon & Way, 2001; Jones, Gilbride-Brown, & Gasiorski, 2005). Stanberry and Azria-Evans (2001) highlight three instructional approaches from which to draw when designing purposeful educational experiences. These approaches are transmission, transaction, and transformation. Transmission is often characterized by conveying facts and knowledge in a lecture format. Transaction has to do with the process of gaining cognitive skills and problem-solving abilities through active inquiry, dialogue/communication, and application of concepts. Transformation facilitates personal and social change through focused discourse, critical reflection, and the application of praxis (learning by doing and reflective action).

These instructional approaches can also be combined to bolster effectiveness. For example, an instructor may lecture about a particular approach or skill for working with older adults (transmission), help students examine personal assumptions and stereotypes about working with older adults and critically evaluate these assumptions through class dialogue (transaction), formulate a plan to implement the skill working with older adults at a community center, reflect on and process the experience (how the plan worked and how the plan was received), and integrate the overall experience into the student's view of working with older adults (transformation).

Critical reflection is a key component of service-learning. When transformation is achieved, the potential for impact is strengthened. Commenting on a service-learning experience in an aging course, Hamon and Way (2001) noted that the "positive effects of service learning were enhanced when students had opportunities to process their experiences with each other in discussions" (p. 82). Deeley (2010), commenting on a service-learning experience in a public policy program stated, "transformation occurred through students challenging their belief systems and assumptions, which led to perspective change" (p. 50). Students in the one of the author's aging classes echo the transformational theme from a service-learning experience working with older adults. Their statements include: "They are just like us: they just look a little older!"; "I was a little afraid to go do my service learning project. I didn't know what to expect exactly but I had so much fun and was pleasantly surprised that I liked being there." and "Some are shy and some are outgoing." Through the experience, students see that many of the beliefs that they held about diverse populations are not true and they spontaneously reevaluate them.

The above instructional methods can serve to help educators create focused and purposeful service-learning experiences where students can learn and discuss course concepts, evaluate preconceived notions and assumptions about the ideas and concepts discussed in the classroom, apply course material in a community/field-based setting, reflect on and process the experience through challenging previously held assumptions, and evaluate new knowledge and skills learned. This experience can aid students in preparation for future internship and professional work. This chapter will describe the various components of a service-learning experience offered through an undergraduate aging course, as well as provide examples for those interested in implementing similar activities and experiences in their area.

16.2 Students Spend Time on Meaningful Tasks

Service-learning as a component of a class experience can be used in a variety of ways. Typically, students are required to serve anywhere from 8 to 20 hours per semester in their site. Instructors sometimes choose to give some release class time for this amount of service but others do not. Many instructors identify specific sites and criteria for service learning. Examples of previous arrangements include:

- placing students in a facility that utilizes art projects for older adults with dementia and spending time working on those projects with an individual after a training period;
- observing individuals with dementia, researching their specific needs, and developing a resource guide for their family; and
- assigning lower-level students to seniors who are already providing service to the community in a supportive role.

For the population of our university, diversity of options of sites and opportunities is critical to meet the needs of our students. Many students are working full time in addition to carrying a full class load. Also, over half of our students live off campus. To require that students work certain hours at a specific site has not worked well for our diverse student population. The course instructor helps provide possible sites and contact numbers, but also gives students the option to propose a suggestion that would work better for them. The goal is for the students to participate in a service-learning project that is meaningful to them as well as to the senior adult with whom they are working and serving. Following this logic, it is critical that connections be drawn between the hands-on experience and course concepts.

16.3 Faculty and Student Peers Interact About Substantive Matters

Whatever service-learning is chosen, the experiences enhance classroom discussions in applying theory and research to specific examples that the students share. Students are able to apply discipline knowledge into their experience. Techniques for reflection may include class assignments that encourage the students to reflect on their experiences in relationship to lifespan changes or developmental domains (physical, emotional, cognitive, and social). Reflections or discussions may focus on how the individual or group they are serving is the norm or exception for their age. Opportunities abound to utilize their service-learning experiences in the classroom and in assignments. Students· may be required to keep a log of hours spent at the site, provide a brief discussion of what was accomplished or observed that day, and receive a signature by someone at the site. Challenges are also part of the equation of planning for service learning. Students need to thoroughly understand the concept before planning their experience, student outcomes must be clear and back up sites or opportunities must be planned in advance.

Service-learning evaluations and assignments should serve as a way to integrate the content of the family life education class' objectives, as well as a way to interchange between transmission, transaction, and transformation methods to enhance the learning environment and the overall experience. Students might choose to work on a project with an older adult such as working on developing a life review for the senior's family or putting together a scrapbook. Through working on the life review with the older adult, students provide significant service by giving a voice to the older adult. The life review whether in written or film format is a gift to the family of the senior adult. The project is also a gift to the student that the elder trusted them with their life history preparation. Child Development or Guidance majors could reflect on their experiences with children by putting together a portfolio of a child's work. Then the portfolio can be shared with the family. Through the experience, the Child Development or Guidance students could reinforce their understanding of the different domains of development for children applying discipline knowledge to the project. Class discussions and evaluation of assignments reflecting on the student's project reinforce the interaction of discipline knowledge and practical application.

16.4 Students Experience Diversity Through Contact with People Different from Themselves

Service-learning encompasses many components of high-impact learning. Students often experience diversity through contact with people who are different than themselves. The experience discussed here is in relation to aging classes. Students work with older adults from a wide range of ethnicities, socioeconomic levels, and backgrounds. Service that students have provided include helping with an event at a retirement center, helping older adults in service to others such as the Alzheimer's Walk, and working together to create a video for recruitment at a senior center. Occasionally, students will also get to work with a different culture or language background. Experiences could match any class within the Family Life Education major.

Students in Child Development classes could work with an agency to put on a bicycle safety training day open to the public. Marriage and Relationship class students could work with a program that provides marriage education or parenting classes. The service-learning experience gives the student opportunities to interact with and experience populations that their personal life might not have included, thus preparing them for the work world. Also, spending time working with different populations and agencies allows networking opportunities for future employment. Students are more clearly able to define their career goals after being exposed to these experiences. Through these experiences, students build valuable relationships, knowledge, and skill sets in preparation for professional work. Ballard and Taylor (2012) note that "competence as a family life educator, as well as cultural competence, comes with practice and experience … varied real-world experiences help to prepare capable family life educators" (p. 292).

Students often enjoy the experience of serving others, making new connections, and seeing that their preconceived concepts of others are incorrect or unsubstantiated. In fact, they have reported that people, regardless of their age or income, are more similar than different through their service-learning experiences. The feedback from agencies, retirement communities, and individuals where students have served is also generally very positive.

The senior adults love interacting with the students. Activities directors and other site coordinators report that the students provide valuable assistance and give the older adults fresh, new interactions that they would not have without the students' participation. Field experiences seem to be a win-win activity for all participants, which support the bi-directional benefits model of service learning. Engaging students and participants in interactions with people different than themselves broadens their knowledge base and world view. Students are, if you will, "required" to experience diversity, which only serves as deeper preparation for working with a variety of individuals and families in the field.

16.5 Activities Have Applications to Different Settings On/Off Campus

There is no limit to the ways that service learning can be conducted. On our campus, we also provide service-learning in our campus child study center. Senior adult volunteers come to campus and serve in the child study center. Our students get the opportunity to serve with the senior adults by working in the child study center. The intergenerational experience thus includes the children, college students, and the senior adults working and playing together. Each generation learns from the other, breaking down negative stereotypes.

Another intergenerational activity that has been well received was a workshop that students helped plan for grandparents raising grandchildren. The purpose of the workshop was to help grandparents realize that college is a possibility with proper planning and knowledge of resources available. Students helped in the planning and execution of this event as well as gave campus tours to the grandchildren and grandparents. They shared study tips and some provided childcare for younger grandchildren so that the grandparents and middle school-aged children could focus on the content of the workshop. The feedback from the grandparents attending this event was very positive, leading to plans to have several more workshops for this population. The students learned significant lessons about diversity through this one event. They also reported learning about some campus resources that they were not aware of themselves.

Volunteer opportunities often evolve from service-learning experiences. In students' written and oral reports, they become very excited about the location where they served. At least 50 % state that they plan to continue in service to the service-learning site. Students' schedules are so busy that working in service-learning hours is challenging, and it is rewarding to know that students find the experience beneficial enough to continue on their own. One student who served at the Alzheimer's Association is now employed there. We have found that employers and prospective employees like to get to know one another before formalizing employment, and service learning provides that opportunity. In some cases, students learn that they do not want to be employed in the location where they did their service-learning hours. Still, that knowledge is valuable for the student and the organization. Providing service-learning opportunities both on and off campus is a venture applicable across all students. Students can then transfer these experiences to future employment and service opportunities.

Conclusion

Service-learning, as a pedagogical tool combining community service and academic study, gives Family Life Educators a means to promote student understanding in many areas. Having students work in the community promotes the integration of theory and research with "real world" experiences, develops their competence as a family educator, and enhances their understanding of culture, gender, and socioeconomic diversity (Brown & Roodin, 2001). Students' awareness of community needs may increase as an outcome of service learning. This awareness can help students be more prepared to plan effective programming when they become Family Life Educators, thus leading to more engaged citizens.

When these experiences are carefully planned and integrated with the course, they provide a transformational opportunity where students not only gain professional skills and knowledge, but also experience personal growth. In summary, service-learning strongly supports many of the tenets of high-impact learning, including spending time on meaningful tasks, faculty and students interacting about the chosen projects, discussing and working with diverse people and situations, and being able to apply the knowledge gained in both on- and off-campus settings.

References

Ballard, S. M., & Taylor, A. C. (2012). *Family life education with diverse populations*. Thousand Oaks, CA: Sage Publications.

Brown, L. A., & Roodin, P. (2001). Service learning in gerontology: An out of classroom experience. *Educational Gerontology, 27*(1), 89–103.

Darling, C. A., Fleming, W. M., & Cassidy, D. (2009). Professionalization of family life education: Defining the field. *Family Relations, 58*, 330–345.

Deeley, S. J. (2010). Service learning: Thinking outside the box. *Active Learning in Higher Education, 11*, 43–53.

Duncan, S. F., & Goddard, H. W. (2011). *Family life education: Principles and practices for effective outreach.* Thousand Oaks, CA: Sage.

Hamon, R. R. (2002). Service learning program pairs, students, elders. *The Older Learner, 10*(3), 4–5.

Hamon, R. R., & Way, C. E. (2001). Integrating intergenerational service learning into Family Science curriculum. *Journal of Teaching in Marriage and Family, 1*, 65–83.

Jones, S., Gilbride-Brown, J., & Gasiorski, A. (2005). Getting inside the underside of service learning: Student resistance and possibilities. In D. W. Butin (Ed.), *Service learning in higher education: Critical issues and directions* (pp. 3–24). Basingstoke, UK: Palgrave Macmillan.

Knapp, J. L., & Stubblefield, P. (2000). Changing students' perceptions of aging: The impact of an intergenerational service learning course. *Educational Gerontology, 26*, 611–621.

Smart, L. S., & Berke, D. L. (2004). Developing professional standards in Family Science internships. *Journal of Teaching in Marriage and Family, 4*, 101–126.

Stanberry, A. M., & Azria-Evans, M. (2001). Perspectives in teaching gerontology: Matching strategies with purpose and context. *Educational Gerontology, 27*, 639–656.

CHAPTER 17

Service Learning in a Helping Skills Course

Jennifer Dobbs-Oates

Service-learning in higher education has been defined and practiced in a variety of ways. Most definitions emphasize two essential components: (1) a service experience based in the community and (2) student learning, which typically includes both applying what has been previously learned to the community setting and reflecting on the service experience to derive additional learning (Jacoby, 1996; Kuh, 2008; Stanton, Giles, & Cruz, 1999). Service-learning has been linked to improved student outcomes in academic achievement, civic engagement, and personal growth (Brownell & Swaner, 2010). Furthermore, students who participate in service-learning activities are also more likely to experience high levels of academic challenge, opportunities for active and collaborative learning and student-faculty interaction, and a supportive campus environment (Kuh, 2008). This chapter will describe one service-learning assignment in detail to examine how service learning can function as a high-impact teaching practice in family science programs.

J. Dobbs-Oates (✉)
Department of Human Development and Family Studies, Purdue University, West Lafayette, IN, USA

17.1 The Service-Learning Assignment

The service-learning project to be explored in this chapter takes place in the Human Development and Family Studies Department at Purdue University, in an upper-division course for students majoring in Human Services. The course is entitled "Skills for Helping Professionals in Individual, Family, and Group Settings," and it is designed to help students develop basic helping skills used by bachelor's-level practitioners of human services (e.g., case managers, parent educators, youth development workers, etc.). These skills include non-verbal communication, active listening, asking questions, communicating empathy, setting goals, and so on.

A major requirement of the course is a multi-step, collaborative service-learning project. The literature on service-learning effectiveness suggests that the strongest outcomes occur when service learning is clearly and closely tied to course content (Brownell & Swaner, 2010; Pascarella & Terenzini, 2005). Accordingly, this project is aligned with a segment of the course focusing on professional helping in a group context. Small student teams work together in partnership with a human services professional who provides services to groups. The objective of the project is for the students to plan one session or meeting of that group. Thus, the project requires that the students apply what they are learning about leading helping groups to the particular group that will be served by their project. Some examples of groups served include a lunchtime mentoring group for at-risk elementary schoolers, an afterschool program for low-income children, a support group for domestic violence survivors, and an educational group for young parents-to-be.

As the project takes place in an upper-division course for majors, it has been intentionally designed as a long-term, multi-step undertaking which gives the student teams a great deal of responsibility for crafting their particular project. The project extends over roughly 12 weeks of the 16-week semester, and the project can be described by dividing it into four phases.

17.1.1 *Phase One*

The first phase involves forming teams, finding community partners, and proposing initial ideas. Teams of four to five students are created by the instructor. The success of the service-learning project depends on the success of the teams in working together; thus, the composition of the teams is crucial. Students typically come to the course having already developed early professional interests in the types of clients they would like to serve, the types of settings they hope to work in, and so forth. When students on a team have overlapping interests, they can plan a service-learning project aligned with those interests, resulting in higher levels of motivation related to the project. Indeed, research on service learning suggests that student interest is a moderating variable associated with better learning outcomes (Astin, Vogelgesang, Ikeda, & Yee, 2000). A useful tool for creating these teams is CATME Smarter Teamwork, a suite of faculty-developed, web-based tools freely available at www.catme.org. The CATME Team-Maker tool allows the course instructor to customize a survey to be completed by the students and use the survey results to build teams. Criteria used to assemble teams for this project include students' interests, schedules, and preferred styles of teamwork.

Once the teams have been identified, students begin working together to identify a community partner for their project. Students are provided with resources to identify potential partners, including a list of community agencies engaged in group-based human services work. However, students are not required to select their partner from that list, nor does the university or instructor set up partnerships in advance. Instead, the students have the responsibility of seeking out potential partners and communicating about the project on their own behalf. This is a substantial responsibility, and would probably not be appropriate for a first-year experience. However, students in this course are typically juniors and seniors and are beginning to plan for their capstone internship and their post-graduation careers. The responsibility of setting up the partnership with the community-based professional is an opportunity to develop and practice important skills in professional communication and networking. Students are given support around this task, including detailed guidelines for making the initial contact and a written agreement to be completed by the students and the professional partner at the outset of the project.

Once the student teams have identified their professional partner, they develop an initial project proposal. This serves as the first written assignment of the project. It is a relatively short, low-stakes assignment designed to give the student teams early feedback on their project ideas. Feedback from the instructor at this stage often catches problems such as failure to comply with assignment objectives and instructions, unrealistic ideas about what can be accomplished in the given time, and lack of understanding of the needs of the agency or client population. This feedback allows students to course correct, resulting in stronger final projects.

17.1.2   *Phase Two*

Next, student teams develop the full proposal for their service-learning project. Perhaps the most important part of this assignment, and certainly the most challenging for the students, is that their proposal must rest on a clear, research-based rationale. Students work with their professional partner to learn more about the needs of the client group they will be serving. They also must search the research literature for information to guide their project. Through this research, they address questions such as: What is known about this topic and this target population? What types of interventions or activities have been effective for similar groups? What do group leaders need to know to be effective in working with this population? Student teams write a short research summary that demonstrates the research evidence for the appropriateness of their planned project. Along with this research summary, they also develop a detailed project proposal including information about the group being served, the topic and procedures of the activity being planned, the objectives of the activity, and any materials to be used. Again, the instructor's feedback on this assignment tends to be quite detailed. In addition to offering guidance on the teams' plans, feedback at this phase is often focused on improving students' research and writing skills.

17.1.3   *Phase Three*

In this phase, the teams carry out the project. In the past, the assignment has allowed student teams to deliver the activity plan and any needed materials to their professional partner, rather than carrying out the activity themselves, if confidentiality issues or other client concerns made it impossible for the students to work directly with the client group. This gave student teams the opportunity to learn about very specialized or high-risk client populations (including victims of domestic violence, court-ordered recipients of substance abuse intervention, etc.). In some cases, this has had very positive outcomes, as students worked in an area of great interest to them and produced some activities and resources that were well-received by professional partners. Unfortunately, this policy was also sometimes abused by student teams, who chose not to conduct their activity with the client group not because of any limitation of the group or professional setting, but because it was just more convenient not to do so. For this reason, the assignment requirements have been changed, and student teams now are required to implement their activity directly with the client group. This is a good example of some of the inevitable trade-offs of field-based experiences in human services and related fields. This decision means that some client groups and professional settings will no longer be appropriate partners for this service-learning project, but it also means that *all* students will get the experience of directly interacting with and leading a group in the community. Service-learning research indicates that direct contact with clients (or, more generally, service recipients) is associated with stronger outcomes for students (Mabry, 1998; Roldan, Strage, & David, 2004). In addition to carrying out their project with their clients, student teams also turn in to the course instructor detailed instructions for their final activity. This demonstrates the final outcome of the various plans and proposals the team turned in at earlier points in the semester.

17.1.4 Phase Four

In the final phase, students engage in both individual and team-based reflection assignments. Evidence suggests that reflection is a key component of a high-quality service-learning experience (Astin et al., 2000; Roldan et al., 2004). Individually, each student writes a short reflection paper about their service-learning experience. These papers cover topics such as lessons learned, course skills/knowledge used in the service project, and the experience of working collaboratively with student teammates and a professional partner. Students engage in weekly reflective writing on other topics throughout the course; thus, this assignment draws on the reflective writing skills students have already developed. This serves as another example of the multiple connections between the service-learning project and the broader course in which it occurs.

As a team, students make a presentation to their fellow classmates that include both a summation of their project and a reflection on the process of engaging in this service-learning activity. This allows students to learn from the other teams in the class, who were working with different professional partners and different client groups. This helps students to learn about the diversity of the human services profession.

The final component of phase four is a self- and peer-evaluation. Students receive an email instructing them to complete the CATME Peer Evaluation, a web-based survey available from the previously described website (www.catme.org). The survey asks students to rate themselves and each of their teammates on a variety of relevant behaviors. This feedback is kept confidential. If consistent feedback depicts unusually strong or weak contributions to the team, that information may be used to adjust individuals' final grades on the service-learning project. Students have expressed appreciation for the opportunity to provide feedback about team functioning. This evaluation step seems to reduce student anxiety related to being graded on a team basis. Additionally, professional partners receive a thank you letter and a feedback survey. Professional partner feedback may also be used to adjust final grades as appropriate.

17.2 High-Impact Features

Service-learning has been identified as a high-impact teaching/learning practice. High-impact practices tend to share certain features that promote student learning and engagement (Kuh, 2008). The specific service-learning assignment described above is a strong example of a high-impact practice. This can be demonstrated by highlighting some of the high-impact features found in this assignment.

17.2.1 *Students Spend Considerable Time on Meaningful Tasks*

Success on this service-learning assignment demands that students spend considerable time on the project. The assignment is a multi-part project with a duration of approximately three-fourths of the semester. Students spend some time in class, and a great deal of time outside of class, working with their teammates on this project. A successful project is likely to require six to eight outside-of-class team meetings over the course of the semester. Students also spend substantial time conducting research, writing, preparing materials, and implementing the project with the client group. The time students spend on this project is not spent on "busy work," but on meaningful tasks. The steps within the project build on one another. Each is necessary to produce the completed final project. What makes these tasks truly meaningful, though, is the fact that students are developing an activity that will be used by a real client group, often a group of people who have some substantial identified need (e.g., victims of domestic violence, children in poverty, pregnant/parenting teens, etc.). This increases student motivation and engagement in the assignment, leading to more substantial and deeper learning.

17.2.2 Students Receive Frequent Performance Feedback

The multi-step nature of this service-learning project is intentionally designed to provide students with multiple opportunities for faculty feedback on their work. Furthermore, by partnering with a human services professional in the community, student teams receive feedback from an experienced, practicing professional throughout the development of their project. Finally, by working together in teams, students receive feedback on their ideas and contributions from their peers. Since feedback is ongoing throughout this long-term project, students have the opportunity to learn from the feedback they receive and to put it to use as they move forward with their project. As a result, students tend to be more engaged in the feedback and more likely to take it seriously as compared to feedback they might receive at the end of a single, stand-alone assignment.

17.2.3 Students Experience Diversity Through Contact with People Who Are Different from Themselves

The most obvious example of this feature is the client group the students are serving through their service-learning project. Client groups served by students in this course have included young, unprepared mothers-to-be; children and teens grieving the loss of a loved one; adults dealing with addiction issues; children living in poverty; and women recovering from experiences of domestic violence. The groups are commonly considered "at risk" in some way and frequently represent a variety of racial, ethnic, socioeconomic, and religious backgrounds. Not only do students interact with these clients by providing a program for them, but they are required first to learn a great deal about their client group and to develop a way in which their project can meet some of the group's needs. This can be a powerful experience for students, not just to have contact with people who are different from themselves, but to develop real empathy for those people.

In addition to the clients, students experience diversity through working with their professional partners and with the other members of their team. A major goal of this project is for the students to learn how to collaborate effectively with a team. To complete the project effectively, students must work closely together over a long period of time. They may discover many differences between themselves and their teammates, but they also discover how to navigate those differences effectively.

17.2.4 Activities Have Applications to Different Settings On/Off Campus

As a field-based experience, this service-learning assignment has clear applications to off-campus settings. Each student team must establish a partnership with a human services professional and develop a program to be used in that person's work setting. Thus, students apply the knowledge and skills they are developing in class to a professional setting in the community. The settings students have worked in have ranged from university-affiliated programs that serve community members, to local human services agencies, to organizations based in the next county. Students have worked in domestic violence shelters, public schools, Head Start programs, community centers, food banks, adult education centers, and more. Not only do they apply their knowledge and skills in the setting they have selected, but they also learn about the work fellow students are doing in other settings through the class presentations.

Conclusion

Service-learning is a high-impact educational practice that has garnered a great deal of attention in higher education over the last couple of decades. Interest in using this practice spans across geographical regions, institution types, and academic disciplines. Service-learning leaders are quick to point out that service learning can be an effective pedagogy in any academic discipline. This is true, but it is also true that we in undergraduate family science programs enjoy some advantages when implementing service-learning programs. The principles of service-learning fit especially well with our field. The knowledge and skills developed in family science programs are ready-made for application to authentic settings. Appropriate settings for service related to family science are plentiful. Reflection, a necessary ingredient in any effective service-learning program, is also a skill essential to family life educators. The example provided in this chapter is but one of many possible applications of service-learning methodology to education in family science. A strong service-learning project will demand a lot of faculty, particularly in the beginning planning stages. However, the potential payoff—in student learning and engagement, in service provided to the community, in connections between the university and professionals practicing in the field—is very large indeed.

References

Astin, A. W., Vogelgesang, L. J., Ikeda, E. K., & Yee, J. A. (2000). *How service learning affects students.* Los Angeles: Higher Education Research Institute.

Brownell, J. E., & Swaner, L. E. (2010). *Five high-impact practices: Research on learning outcomes, completion, and quality.* Washington, DC: Association of American Colleges and Universities.

Jacoby, B. (1996). Service-learning in today's higher education. In B. Jacoby (Ed.), *Service-learning in higher education: Concepts and practices* (pp. 3–25). San Francisco: Jossey-Bass.

Kuh, G. D. (2008). *High-impact educational practices: What they are, who has access to them, and why they matter.* Washington, DC: Association of American Colleges and Universities.

Mabry, J. B. (1998). Pedagogical variations in service-learning and student outcomes: How time, contact and reflection matter. *Michigan Journal of Community Service, 5,* 32–47.

Pascarella, E. T., & Terenzini, P. T. (2005). *How college affects students: A third decade of research* (Vol. 2). San Francisco: Jossey-Bass.

Roldan, M., Strage, A., & David, D. (2004). A framework for assessing academic service-learning across disciplines. In M. Welch & S. H. Billig (Eds.), *New perspectives in service-learning: Research to advance the field* (pp. 39–59). Greenwich, CT: Information Age Publishing.

Stanton, T. K., Giles, D. E., & Cruz, N. I. (1999). *Service learning: A movement's pioneers reflect on its origins, practice, and future.* San Francisco: Jossey-Bass.

CHAPTER 18

Teaching Grant Writing to Undergraduate Students: A High-Impact Experience

Bryce L. Jorgensen, Sharon M. Ballard, Eboni Baugh, Alan Taylor, and Elizabeth Carroll

The Family and Community Services (FCS) program at East Carolina University (ECU) is an undergraduate degree program designed to prepare students to work with individuals and families or systems across the lifespan. Many FCS graduates work in non-profit child and family agencies where fundraising has always been important but has become even more critical in these challenging economic times. Fundraising includes events ranging from car washes to dinners with auctions or writing proposals to grant-making agencies. In order for students to be successfully employed, it is important to recognize that in addition to client-based skills, students need sustainability skills such as fundraising and grant writing(Wark, 2008).

B.L. Jorgensen (✉)
Department of Extension Family and Consumer Sciences, New Mexico State University, Las Cruces, NM, USA

S.M. Ballard • A. Taylor • E. Carroll
Department of Human Development and Family Science, East Carolina University, Greenville, NC, USA

E. Baugh
Department of Human Development and Family Science, East Carolina University, Greenville, NC, USA

Community-based learning experiences can facilitate skills training and practical hands-on learning translates into well-prepared professionals that have the skill set to be successful in the workplace and to make a positive difference for families (Griffith, Hart, & Goodling, 2006; Taylor & Ballard, 2012). The purpose of this chapter is to describe how competencies in fundraising are incorporated into the FCS curriculum and to describe the methods we use to teach the grant-writing process.

Students in FCS take a course entitled "Theory and Practice in Family and Community Services." This course is part of a sequence of courses designed to effectively prepare students through progressively more complex and challenging service-learning components. We provide an overview of fundraising including types of fundraising, why people give, and how to maximize fundraising activities. This information then is applied through two service-learning projects. The first is to participate in a fundraising activity with an agency or organization, which can include face-to-face involvement with activities such as a rock-a-thon, bake sale, or a large event like a fashion show. Students may help with the organization, marketing, or implementation of the fundraising activity.

The second service-learning project, writing a grant proposal for a community partner, is the main focus of this chapter. We will address identifying and working with community partners, the writing and peer-review process, reflection, and presentation. We conclude with recommendations and quotes from students who have completed the course projects. Throughout the chapter, we illustrate how this experience meets the following elements of a high-impact experience for students: (1) students spend considerable amounts of time on the meaningful tasks, (2) faculty and student peers interact about substantive matters, (3) students receive frequent performance feedback, (4) activities have applications to different settings on/off campus, and (5) authentic connections are made with peers, faculty, community, and/or the university (Kuh, 2008).

18.1 COMMUNITY PARTNERS

Writing a grant proposal for an actual project with a real community partner is an authentic experience that allows students to become more passionate than if they wrote a proposal for a hypothetical project.

Typically, we work with a community partner around a specific project or program. In this way, the grant-writing *activities have applications to different settings on/off campus* and students are exposed to a variety of community needs and programs that meet those needs. Community partners for the grant-writing portion of the course are selected by the instructors based on both the community partner need and the fit with the course objectives. We choose community partners for whom it will be a mutually beneficial experience and we try to clearly communicate both benefits and expectations for the partnership. We ask partners to present to the class about their agency and specific funding needs and to be available to answer follow-up questions that arise throughout the semester. At the end of the semester, we are able to share electronic copies of the proposals with the partner and they are able to combine, revise, and tweak the proposals to fit specific funding guidelines. The service-learning component of this project allows for *authentic connections to be made with peers, faculty, community, and the university.*

We have worked with a variety of community partners representing a wide range of agencies and programs within our community. One example was an agency called Building Hope who identified two funding needs: ReCycle, a program to help young men gain job skills and Women of Worth (WOW), which helps young women graduate from high school and continue in college or employment. The class was divided into six groups (three per program) with four students per group. This approach of multiple groups per funding need can be beneficial to the community partner in that they have multiple proposals from which they can choose or combine various elements. Another example was the pediatric palliative care program at the local hospital. This program had many different funding needs including training programs, memory boxes for families whose child died, a children's palliative care room, a bereavement ceremony for families, etc. In this example, we had several groups of four or five students each working on a different funding need. This breadth can be beneficial for those partners with many different projects or programs. The key is to identify specific funding areas that truly meet the community partner needs. However, as program planning is a different skill, the instructor should be sure that the funding is needed for an existing program or one that has already been developed. Otherwise, students may focus more on program planning rather than the grant writing.

18.2 THE WRITING AND PEER-REVIEW PROCESS

The process used to teach grant writing within this course has evolved over time, and each instructor implements the process in a slightly different way. One of us spreads the grant-writing project throughout the semester interspersing the steps into the other course material. This approach reinforces grant writing as a process and ensures adequate time to teach, write, review, and revise each step. The other instructor covers the grant-writing project in a six-week block of the semester. This more intensive approach allows students to focus solely on the project and to avoid diluting it with other course material. Either approach results in *students spending considerable amounts of time on the meaningful tasks* involved in grant writing.

Two sections of this course with 25–35 students each are taught every semester with an instructor typically teaching one section and working with a specific community partner. It is not helpful for our community partner to receive 25–35 grant proposals; yet, the course carries writing intensive credit. This makes it important to have each student write and demonstrate competence with all components of a grant proposal. Consequently, we use a combination of individual and group writing. Through the community partner's discussion of their program and specific funding needs, we generate a list of topics or funding areas. Groups are formed around these topics with four to five students per group.

The grant proposal is grouped into components: organization background, needs statement, goals and objectives, methods, evaluation, sustainability, and budget. Each component is covered in the text used for the class (Carlson & O'Neal-McElarth, 2008). After the students read the chapter, the component is discussed in class and then the group works together to discuss and gather necessary information. *Students receive frequent performance feedback* on their work from the instructor and from peers. Each student writes these grant components individually and after completing one or two components, students bring a copy for review by another student from a different group. Peer review allows students to benefit from additional feedback on their work and to learn from reviewing and critiquing others' work. Some instructors have found it beneficial to organize the class as a review committee, with each student serving as primary and secondary reviewer of another student's proposals (Wooley, 2004). However, we organize it so our students have three opportunities to give and receive feedback, receiving credit for both their writing and their ability to provide feedback which increases the quality of the peer-review process. Students often comment that by learning what to look for when reviewing another student's proposal, they better understand the strengths and weaknesses of their own proposal.

Ultimately, students use the feedback they received from their peers and instructor to work with their group to integrate and synthesize all the best ideas and feedback into one proposal. The synthesized, completed grant proposal is peer reviewed one more time. By the end of the semester, each student has written and provided feedback on the individual steps and the full grant proposal. Furthermore, each group has one grant proposal that is written specifically for their funding topic and they have received feedback from peers and instructor numerous times. Students must write each component of the grant proposal individually in order to received credit for the group proposal. With this process, the community partner receives 6–8 proposals as opposed to 25–35! Additionally, each student is learning about each component and they benefit from the synergy that develops within the groups. For example, each group member may approach their needs statement differently and by combining the best of each, they end up with a stronger needs statement. The whole really is greater than the sum of the parts!!

18.3 Reflection and Presentation

Reflection is incorporated into the course in three ways: discussion, a guided reflection paper, and a presentation. Throughout the course, students reflect on the community partner, the audience served, and specific aspects of programming through the actual writing of the grant components, discussion with classmates, and through the feedback process. Through writing the various components of a grant proposal, students come to understand the community, the target audience in question, and the role of the community partner in filling community needs. This understanding is much more thorough and nuanced than simply talking about a particular agency or community issue. The students put themselves in the shoes of the community partner and come to feel the passion for the target audience or the issue about which they are writing. Throughout the process, the discussions, reflection activities, and group work allow *faculty and student peers to interact about substantive matters*. Faculty, students, and community partners work together to discuss community needs, resources, and solutions.

The second reflection opportunity comes at the end of the semester through a reflection paper in which students describe their community fundraising experience, reflect on the role of fundraising within family and community services, and compare and contrast their community fundraising experience with their grant-writing experience. This reflection activity allows the student to see grant writing in the context of fundraising and the role that grant writing plays in the field of family and community services.

The final reflection opportunity is a presentation. Not only is presenting an important mode of reflection, but effectively presenting one's ideas is a necessary skill when working with individuals and families in the community (Taylor & Ballard, 2012) and with potential funders. After a discussion on where to find different types of grants, each group finds three potential funders for their specific grant. At the end of the semester, students present their grant proposals to their community partner and/or their classmates as if they were presenting to one of the three potential funders they found and persuading them to fund the project. To help them succeed, each student takes a prerequisite communications course in which they learn the theories and principles of public speaking and giving presentations. We also review and discuss tips for giving a group presentation. Students have to be professionally dressed and stand in the front of the class (not surround the podium). They present to the class as if their classmates are the funders and present their grant proposal with the goal of getting funded. Community partners can be invited to the presentation as well which adds an additional level of authenticity to the presentation. The presentations are recorded and students have an opportunity to review their presentations. Students critique their presentation style and speaking skills. Eisenberg (2003) reiterates that students have an opportunity to reflect on what they could have done better, what they learned, and what was most helpful about the experience. Presenting the proposals allows students to think through each step of the grant process one more time which tends to solidify the grant components in their brain. Additionally, the presentation allows students to practice their persuasive presentation skills and to implement the important aspects of fundraising helping the audience feel a connection to the need.

18.4 A High-Impact Experience for Students

Grant writing is an important skill for students pursuing a career in family life education, and writing real proposals for a community partner results in a high-impact experience for students. Overall, students have recognized this impact and have responded positively to the grant-writing experience. Although it is challenging, they appreciate the method that we use to break down the process.

> I thought the grant writing process was very helpful. I was freaking out when I found out that we would be writing a grant, but when it was broken down in steps it didn't make it feel like it was so much. Working in groups and the peer reviews were really helpful as well.

Others recognize the value of grant writing as a necessary skill and appreciate being able to work with a real community partner.

> I think that writing a grant in class is the major strength. It will help us in our future jobs. Part of my internship next semester is helping the agency write grants. I feel that this class has prepared me for it, and will also look good on my resume for future jobs.
>
> I have particularly enjoyed the grant writing assignment. It is always most beneficial to me to participate in an assignment where I feel that I am truly making a difference and can see the effects of my work.

18.5 Recommendations

1. Set your students up for success. At the beginning, students feel overwhelmed by the task of writing a grant proposal for a community partner. Reassure them that writing a grant proposal is not easy, but is something they can do successfully! Divide the grant proposal into manageable sections and lead them step by step through the process.
2. Use a grading rubric. Students need clear expectations about each portion of the process and how they will be evaluated. Use the same rubric for the peer review that you use to assign grades on the final proposal to reinforce review criteria.
3. Facilitate effective group work. In order to facilitate a positive group experience and hold students accountable for their own work, use a group rating form that allows students to evaluate each group members' performance and to document specific member contributions to the project.
4. Identify appropriate community partners and funding needs. Funding for programs rather than operating costs or capital campaigns are more conducive to this project. The community partner must identify funding needs that are part of an existing program or a program that has been planned but has lacked funding for implementation. Program planning involves a different skill set and is beyond the scope of the course.

5. Foster clear and ongoing communication with community partners about expectations. The community partner must be willing to provide information about their agency and the specific funding needs. This is to ensure that in exchange, we are able to provide them with grant proposals that will actually meet their funding needs.

Conclusion

Writing a grant proposal is a challenging task. Teaching undergraduate students to write a grant proposal is even more challenging! It can also be a bit scary when you know that you will be sharing your students work with your community partner. However, the effort is well worth the results. If given the opportunity, students will rise to the challenge and produce, not only a grant proposal of which they and you as the instructor can be proud, but a proposal that can be a vehicle for making a difference in the lives of families in your community.

References

Carlson, M., & O'Neal-McElarth, T. (2008). *Grant writing: Step by step* (5th ed.). San Francisco, CA: Jossey-Bass/John Wiley & Sons, Inc..

Eisenberg, T. (2003). Teaching successful grant writing to psychology graduate students. *Teaching of Psychology, 30,* 328–330.

Griffith, J. D., Hart, C. L., & Goodling, M. M. (2006). Teaching grant writing with service learning. *International Journal of Teaching and Learning in Higher Education, 18,* 222–229. Retrieved from http://www.isetl.org/ijtlhe/ ISSN 1812-9129.

Kuh, G. D. (2008). *High-impact educational practices: What they are, who has access to them, and why they matter.* Association of American Colleges and Universities. Retrieved from http://www.neasc.org/downloads/aacu_high_impact_2008_final.pdf

Taylor, A. C., & Ballard, S. M. (2012). Preparing students to work with diverse populations. In S. M. Ballard & A. C. Taylor (Eds.), *Family life education with diverse populations* (pp. 285–302). Thousand Oaks, CA: Sage Publications Inc.

Wark, L. J. (2008). Introduction to grant writing for undergraduates. *Human Services Today,* 5(1), online. Retrieved from http://opus.ipfw.edu/humser_facpubs/5

Wooley, S. F. (2004). A review committee as a way to teach grant writing skills. *American Journal of Health Education, 35*(6), 366–368. Retrieved from http://dx.doi.org/10.1080/19325037.2004.10604777

CHAPTER 19

Conclusion

Ashley Schmitt

High-Impact Practices (HIP) in the form of field-based learning have been and are continuing to be emphasized in Family Life Education and Family Science programs. These programs are well suited to field-based learning as they typically require some type of actual in the community/workplace experience while being guided by instructors and on-site supervisors. Field-based learning is also an excellent vehicle for Family Science programs to transform knowledge and skills into practice. Infusing field-based course work with high-impact elements enhances the experience for students by creating authentic, collaborative, impactful experiences. But while the literature is filled with the benefits of such experiences, there is a lack of information on how to incorporate these experiences into the classroom. This manuscript is designed to help fill that gap and the preceding pages contain examples of how each author incorporated this pedagogical idea into their courses. But to this end, how each institution and educator structures and forms the experiences for students is different but with some key commonalities that make the experiences high impact:

A. Schmitt (✉)
Office of Graduate and Professional Studies, Texas A&M University, College Station, TX, USA

- they demand that students devote a considerable amount of time and effort to a purposeful task;
- students interact with faculty and peers about substantive matters;
- students receive frequent and meaningful feedback;
- students have opportunities to see how what they are learning applies in different settings, on and off campus;
- students experience diversity through contact with people who are different from themselves (Kuh, 2008);
- connect personally and professionally through opportunities for active, collaborative learning (AAC&U, 2007).

Finally, all of the experiences described here are grounded in theory.

In this work, field-based learning is separated by treatment as either by course as the experience or by experience in the course. The first section deals with the course as the experience and is divided further by either a practicum or internship experience while the second section deals with experience in the course and is separated into either a service-learning or community-based experience. While some instructors develop the experience as an internship or practicum, others create the experience around a service-learning project or community-based experience. They all incorporate the common high-impact elements and are based in theory. There is no one way or "correct" way to structure a high-impact experience as illustrated by the authors in this work but each is effective by taking into consideration the institution and student population as well as community partners and incorporating high-impact elements into their practice.

The first section of this book deals with the treatment of internships and practicums (the course as the experience), employing elements to make each experience high-impact in nature. As defined by Kuh (2008), the internship experience provides students with direct experience in the field with the benefit of supervision and coaching from a professional that culminates in a final event/paper/project. The internship and practicum experiences created by the instructors in these pages are different in structure and focus but share commonalities in the form of HIP elements.

Internship discussion focuses on:

- Three course sequence culminating in an internship experience;
- In-house procedure to match students and Internship sites through a ten-step process;

- On-campus event connecting students to community agencies that is integrated into pre-internship and internship courses;
- Teaching observation and how to interpret behaviors in two courses;
- Modified teaching of Family Life Education methodology with a focus on the class, the certification, and the experience;
- And reflection and feedback.

While all employ HIP elements, they may only employ a few of the HIP elements. The main high-impact elements incorporated into the internship experiences discussed included frequent feedback, applications on/off campus, diversity, and time spent on task were the most frequently cited.

The practicum experience before the internship is an important step to prepare students in Family Sciences programs for field experiences. Typically, a practicum experience is an experience in which theory is put into practice.

Practicum discussion focused on:

- Sixty hours each at two sites and gain life span experience and professional skills using tools such as reflection through journaling and conducting an investigative interview of the agency and a professional in the field;
- And an introductory field experience course that incorporates field work, experiential activities, structured journaling, and work group learning communities.

No matter how the practicum experience is formatted, they are based in theory and have high-impact elements woven into the experience. Through all the discussions, the high-impact elements that were most frequently cited were experiencing diversity, time spent on meaningful tasks, authentic connections, applications on/off campus, and frequent performance feedback.

The second section of this book deals with the treatment of service-learning and community-based experiences (experience in the course) to employ elements to make each experience high-impact in nature. Service-learning and community-based experiences, in Family Science programs, are another vehicle for students to explore concepts and skills important to the field. Kuh (2008) describes these types of programs of field-based experiential learning as an instructional part of the course where students receive direct experience with issues they are studying in the course and analyzing and creating solutions to problems. He identifies key features of this type of practice as students have the opportunity to both apply what they are learning to the real world and reflect in the classroom on their experience (Kuh, 2008). In this work, discussion of service-learning featured concepts such as:

- Exploring how Family Life Education can benefit communities through preventative programming;
- Re-designing a course to transform student motivation;
- Using reverse planning to design a field-based experience;
- Designing a project working backwards and using the Management Model to form teams and place students with community agencies;
- The instructional level of planning a project highlighting transmission, transaction, and transformation;
- And a multi-step collaborative service-learning project in an upper-division course.

Community-based experience discussion featured ideas such as:

- Two courses aligned with high-impact elements and NAEYC standards focusing on structure of the courses and student assignments;
- Students working in inter-professional team with local human service community organizations to create programming;
- Teaching fundraising and grant writing process by identifying and working with community partners.

Again, not all high-impact elements were identified by instructors as being integrated into the experience. Typically, an average of four elements were identified as being incorporated into the experience though all were most likely present. Most often cited as being integrated into service-learning and community-based experiences were time on tasks, frequent performance feedback, interacting about substantive matters, and application to different settings on/off campus.

The field-based experiences presented in this work are only a small collection of ideas that can be designed and implemented that incorporate high-impact elements and give students an authentic, active experience. It was designed to contribute to the literature and present the plethora of possibilities when it comes to high-impact experiences for students. There is no template for implementing high-impact practices in the classroom. For each instructor, how the experience is designed, integrated, and executed will be different based on a number of factors. These are not one-size-fits-all models and are only guides to the experiences that can be created for students in Family Sciences programs.

REFERENCES

American Association of Colleges and Universities (AAC&U). (2007). *College learning for the new global century: A report from the national leadership council for liberal education and America's promise*. Washington, DC: Association of American Colleges and Universities.

Kuh, G. (2008). *High-impact educational practices: What they are, who has access to them, and why they matter*. Washington, DC: AAC&U Publishing.

Appendix A: Writing Assignment Questions from the Role of Practicum in Undergraduate Family Life Education

Writing Assignment Questions

Each student is required to prepare the following material as part of the practicum experience and must be completed for both of the practicum experiences.

1. Name of agency or service organization
2. Address
3. Supervisor's name and title
4. Mission and purpose of the service organization
5. Funding and staffing:

    (a) Source of funds
    (b) Approximate annual budget
    (c) Number of staff

    - Total
    - Professional
    - Clerical
    - Other

    (d) Organizational chart. If there is no available chart, prepare one with the help of your supervisor.

6. Select a professional at the bachelor's degree level. Interview the person and describe the job duties and responsibilities of the individual.
7. Present a brief history of the agency; describe the current problems it tends to have to address.
8. What are the stated goals of the agency? Explain how family studies professionals might contribute toward the achievement of these goals.
9. Describe the networking process of the agency. To whom does it typically refer clients? For what purposes are such referrals usually made?
10. Describe your specific duties and how they relate to the overall goals of the agency.
11. Describe the range of clients served by the agency. Include general demographic data concerning the age, gender, race, income level, housing, occupation, education, rural-urban, family structure, and any other data you deem relevant.
12. Compare the income level of your agency's clients with data on average national/regional income levels. Use actual data and identify sources.
13. Interview staff people on both the bachelor's and master's degree levels, using the guidelines below:

    (a) Name
    (b) School where advanced degree was obtained
    (c) Experience in the field
    (d) Why they choose a helping profession?
    (e) Why they decide that an advanced degree was needed?
    (f) Describe their current assignment and duties

Appendix B: Rubrics, Assignments, Evaluations, and Reflections from Community-Based Learning with Young Children in a Child Development Center

Child Development

Group Project

Portfolio
1. Submit a collection of the items/work examples listed below, arranged in a professional, attractive binder. It must be <u>well organized</u>, easy to read for the instructor. Table of Contents page does not require page numbers to be listed, but must be color coded to the entry sections.
2. Section dividers with colored tabs and sheet protectors are required. Each <u>page</u> must be visible through a sheet protector. Instructor will not pull out pages for viewing.
3. <u>Order of placement in binder:</u>
    (a) Title page with child's picture
    (b) Disclaimer page with group member info
    (c) Table of Contents
    (d) Background history of the child (Information from parent interview)
        - Full name
        - Birth date
        - Family info (e.g., parents married, child lives with both parents)

- Sibling info (e.g., child is youngest with 4 siblings)
- Health history (e.g., normal birth, premature birth, etc.)

    (e) Anecdotal records

- Rough drafts (4 per person)
- Final drafts (4 per person)

    (f) Standards checklist

- Completed checklist
- Visual documentation (securely attached with rubber cement)

Identify the standard that is being evidenced in the photo
at least 12 photos (3-4 per person)
the more the better

    (g) Work samples (gathered from lab staff)

- Written samples
- Artwork samples

    (h) Parent interview

- Summary from each group member

    (i) Narrative reports

- One of each per group member

Rough draft
Final draft

Elements	Especially high-quality work	Good, solid work	Needs strengthening	Needs significantly more work	Especially high-quality work
Professional format • Binder • Title page • Disclaimer page • Color dividers • Typed labels • Sheet protectors • Table of contents • Easy to navigate	Especially high-quality work, well thought out	Good, solid work, nice work	Needs strengthening, needs work/reformatting Missing items, incomplete	Needs significantly more work, inaccurate, poor quality or condition	Majority of items not included, extremely poor quality, disorganized
Background history of child • Full name • Birth date • Family info • Sibling info • Health history	Especially high-quality work, well thought out	Good, solid work, nice work	Needs strengthening, needs work/reformatting Missing items, incomplete	Needs significantly more work, inaccurate, poor quality or condition	Majority of items not included, extremely poor quality
Anecdotal records rough drafts included • 4 per each member of group	All anecdotal rough drafts included	Majority of anecdotal rough drafts included	Some of the anecdotal rough drafts included	Few of the anecdotal rough drafts included	None included
Final anecdotal records • 4 per each member of group	All anecdotal final drafts included	Majority of anecdotal final drafts included	Some of the anecdotal final drafts included	Few of the anecdotal final drafts included	None included
Early Learning Standards checklist	100 items observed and documented	75 items observed and documented	50 items observed and documented	25 items observed and documented	Less than 25 items observed and documented

Criteria				
Visual documentation • Minimum of 12 • Early Learning Standards identified • Securely attached on pages • In sheet protectors	More than 12 included	10–12 included	7–9 included	4–6 included	Less than 4 included
Children's work samples • Minimum of 5 • Standards identified • In sheet protectors	More than 5 included	4–5 included	3 included	1–2 included	No samples included
Parental interview • Each group member attended the interview session • Summary included (1 per group member)	Each group member attended the interview session, each group member arrived on time and was professional All summaries included	Majority of the group members attended the interview session, majority of the group members arrived on time and were professional Majority of summaries included	Some of the group members attended the interview session, some of the group members arrived on time and were professional Some of summaries are included	Few of the group members attended the interview session, few of the group members arrived on time and were professional Few of summaries are included	No interview was conducted
Mechanics • Correct grammar • No typos • Professionally written	Especially high-quality work, correct grammar, no typos, professionally written	Good, solid work, nice grammar, one to two typos, professionally written	Needs strengthening, needs work, grammar adequate, several typos, colloquialisms used, writing too casual	Needs significantly more work, poor quality or condition, many typos, incorrect grammar, writing too casual, many colloquialisms used throughout paper	Extremely poor quality work

CHILD DEVELOPMENT

Group Project

Portfolio Rubric

Child Development

Individual Project

Narrative Report Directions

Writing a narrative report involves you systematically reviewing the contents of the portfolio and correlating children's activities to extrinsic standards.

Narrative reports do not have to be lengthy (ten to twelve paragraphs is sufficient) but they should be thorough. The report needs to summarize the child's growth, development, and academic achievements. A common mistake is to devote an entire narrative report to a child's behavior.

You MUST include the following in your narrative report:

- Introduction
- Summary of child's progress
- Key developments in child's progress
  - Cognitive Development

Mathematical Development
Science Development
Social Studies Development

  - Creative Arts Development
  - Health and Physical Development
  - Language and Literacy
  - Social and Emotional Development

- Reflection on child's development, including strengths and weaknesses observed
- Conclusion

1. Review the contents in the child's portfolio and make notes for each section of the report. Some items will yield information for just one section; others will relate to several sections.
2. Draft a thesis statement or main point for each section. Number your comments about various portfolio items that you want to use as back-up for your thesis statement.
3. Ask yourself, "Is any pattern or trend apparent?" Draft these observations, if any, for the summary.
4. Write the sections.
5. Read the sections aloud to yourself or a friend. Do they make sense? While reading did you stop or pause at a place where you should not have? This is a clue that maybe the sentence needs to be reworked.
6. Ask yourself, "Have I overlooked any important areas? Do I need to plan systematic observations or other techniques to assess this child's development in those areas?" Note any plans for future assessment.
7. Edit. Edit. Edit.
8. Proofread. Beware of homophones!
9. Turn in rough draft 1 by:_____
10. Turn in rough draft 2 by:_____
11. Turn in final draft by:_____
12. Put rough draft and final draft in the child's portfolio.

CHILD DEVELOPMENT

Individual Project

Narrative Report Rubric

APPENDIX B 207

Elements	Especially high-quality work	Good, solid work	Needs strengthening	Needs significantly more work

Organization of paper
APA style*
Coversheet
Margins, indention of paragraphs
Double spaced
Running headers (upper right hand corner), with page numbers
Headings (within text)
  Centered
  Upper and lower case
  No hanging headers
Print only on front side of paper
*Refer to APA manual
	All directions for organizing and submitting the report were followed and adhered to in all areas	Two directions for organizing and submitting the report were not followed and adhered to	Directions for organizing and submitting the report were partially followed and adhered to in all areas	Directions for organizing and submitting the report were not followed and adhered to in several areas

Introduction (1) Begins with a topic sentence that introduces a general theme. (2) Follows the topic sentence with sentences that narrow the focus of the theme, so that it is less general. (3) Introduces the child of the text you are writing about. (4) Narrows the discussion of the topic by identifying what the reader will read in the upcoming paragraphs. (5) Finishes by making a debatable claim a thesis statement, which is defined as a debatable point/claim. Always locate the thesis statement as the final sentence of the introductory paragraph.	Especially high-quality work, well thought out	Good, solid work, nice work	Needs strengthening, needs work/reformatting Missing items, incomplete (shows little improvement)	Needs significantly more work, inaccurate (shows no improvement), poor quality or condition, limited examples

Section	Exceptional	Good	Needs Strengthening	Needs Significant Work
1st body paragraph — Summary of child's progress — Short synopsis of how the child has grown over the past couple of months	Especially high-quality work, well thought out	Good, solid work, nice work	Needs strengthening, needs work/reformatting Missing items, incomplete (shows little improvement)	Needs significantly more work, inaccurate (shows no improvement), poor quality or condition, limited examples
Subsequent body paragraphs — Key developments in child's progress; Identify Early Learning Standards and link to observations to discuss examples of progress in each area. Cognitive Development, Mathematical, Science, Social Studies, Creative Arts, Health and Physical, Language and Literacy, Social and Emotional	Early Learning Standards clearly identified and linked to several examples Content reflects effort, thought, and planning in all areas to an exceptional degree	Early Learning Standards identified and linked to some examples Content reflects effort, thought, and planning in most areas	Early Learning Standards not clearly identified, limited examples or not linked to Early Learning Standards Content partially reflects effort, thought, and planning	Early Learning Standards not identified, little to no examples used or not linked to Early Learning Standards Content does not reflect effort, thought, and planning

Reflection Reflection on child's development, including strengths and weaknesses observed	Early Learning Standards clearly identified and linked to several examples Content reflects effort, thought, and planning in all areas to an exceptional degree	Early Learning Standards identified and linked to some examples Content reflects effort, thought, and planning in most areas	Early Learning Standards not clearly identified, limited examples or not linked to Early Learning Standards Content partially reflects effort, thought, and planning	Early Learning Standards not identified, little to no examples used or not linked to Early Learning Standards Content does not reflect effort, thought, and planning
Conclusion (1) Begins with a topic sentence that clearly relates to the topic that was identified in the introductory paragraph. (2) Sentences that make connections with, or revisit, points from your introductory paragraph and your body paragraphs. These points now serve to close your argument. (3) A synthesis of these points that clearly demonstrates the focus of your thesis statement. (4) A final comment, or intellectual conclusion of sorts that points out the larger significance of your argument.	Especially high-quality work, well thought out	Good, solid work, nice work	Needs strengthening, needs work/reformatting Missing items, incomplete (shows little improvement)	Needs significantly more work, inaccurate (shows no improvement), poor quality or condition, limited examples

Criterion	Excellent	Good	Needs Improvement	Poor
This should be embedded throughout the body paragraphs. Making generalizations and supporting them with evidence:	Providing appropriate examples and quotations to support the main points you are making, with extended discussion	Providing appropriate examples and quotations to support points you are making with substantial discussion	Providing some examples and quotations but not for all points or with limited discussion	Providing few examples and quotations
This should be evident through the various drafts turned into the teacher Revising *Graded in RD#2 & Final	Substantially reseeing, reorganizing, and rearranging elements of essays as you work through different drafts, using responses from readers to add, expand, clarify, restructure	Doing some reshaping in different drafts giving consideration to readers' responses	Making primarily minor changes or additions between drafts, with little reshaping giving occasional consideration to readers' responses	Making few changes between drafts not responding to readers' comments
This should be evident through the various drafts turned into the teacher Editing and Proofreading: *Graded in RD#2 and Final	Always rereading carefully for • clarity of sentences • conventions of academic written texts • Proofreading	Generally rereading carefully. Generally correct conventions and clean text and/or using appropriate strategies to improve these areas	Not always editing and proofreading carefully. Not consistently using strategies to improve these areas	No real effort at improving sentence clarity, consistently using appropriate conventions, proofreading, or using strategies to improve these areas
Mechanics • Correct grammar • Correct spelling • No typos • Correct punctuation • Clear, flowing text • Professionally written (no contractions, no slang, not casual writing)	Especially high-quality work, correct grammar, no typos, professionally written	Good, solid work, nice grammar, one to two typos, professionally written	Needs strengthening, needs work, grammar adequate, several typos, colloquialisms used, writing too casual	Needs significantly more work, poor quality or condition, many typos, incorrect grammar, writing too casual, many colloquialisms used throughout paper

Environments for Young Children

Student Weekly Reflection

1. What emerging knowledge, skills, and dispositions did you observe in a child or children today?

2. What learning occurred without your direct intervention?

3. What learning occurred with your intervention?

4. Give <u>specific</u> examples that illustrate what the child did and what you did.

5. How do you know that the children understood the concept? Give <u>specific</u> examples of individual children to which you taught the concept.

6. How did the child (children) respond to you?

7. What went well? What didn't?

8. How could you have strengthened this experience (planning, presentation, material)?

9. After this experience, what changes might you make?

10. Ideas or plans that might provoke further growth.

Environments for Young Children

Lab Practicum Weekly Evaluation

Presentation of Self

- Punctual & dependable
- Calm
- Enthusiastic
- Engaged
- Professional
- Prepared
- Self-assured
- Exhibits insight
- Asks questions for clarification
- Participates in activities
- Leaves when dismissed, not any earlier
- Professionally dressed in uniform

____Especially high quality
____Good, solid, work
____Needs strengthening
____Needs significantly more work
____Does not exhibit these qualities

Interaction with Team

- Checks in/out with Manager
- Carries share of load
- Shows initiative
- Supportive of other team members
- Helpful to team members
- Models socially acceptable behaviors

____Especially high quality
____Good, solid, work
____Needs strengthening
____Needs significantly more work
____Does not exhibit these qualities

Lab Knowledge

- Concerned with Health & Safety Issues
- Knows & follows Procedures (snack; bathroom; set up/ clean up; outdoors; assignment; circle time)
- Checks lesson plans & sets up area
- Models appropriate language, speaks clearly and distinctly
- Positions self so all areas of the room/playground are easily visible
- Sits behind the children at group time and attend to the children as needed
- Returns materials to storage, straightens shelves, check supplies, and cleans surfaces

____Especially high quality
____Good, solid, work
____Needs strengthening
____Needs significantly more work
____Does not exhibit these qualities

Interaction with Staff

- Understands/ follows directions
- Accepts & makes use of suggestions
- Asks appropriate questions
- Respectful
- Models socially acceptable behavior (tactful behavior, manners, etc.)

____Especially high quality
____Good, solid, work
____Needs strengthening
____Needs significantly more work
____Does not exhibit these qualities

Interactions with Children

- Problem-solving/ encourages independence
- Enjoys children
- Empathetic
- Observes needs
- Respects possessions
- Converses appropriately
- Listens attentively to children
- Gently reminds children of class rules (be safe, be neat, be kind), "Use indoor voices"
- Encourages children's efforts with verbal reinforcements such as "I see you are very proud of yourself"
- Attempts to sit, kneel, or bend at child's level when talking or listening to children
- Encourages children to clean up area

____Especially high quality
____Good, solid, work
____Needs strengthening
____Needs significantly more work
____Does not exhibit these qualities

Additional Notes

Environments for Young Children

Lab Practicum

End of Semester Evaluation

1. ATTENDANCE:

    (a) Perfect attendance
    (b) 1 absence
    (c) 2 absences
    (d) 3 absences
    (e) 4 or more absences

2. PUNCTUALITY:

    (a) Always on time/never leaves early
    (b) Late once/leaves early once
    (c) Late twice/leaves early twice
    (d) Late more than twice/leaves early more than twice

3. ATTITUDE:
Interested in children, positive interactions with children, positive with adults and children, welcomes and uses suggestions.

    (a) Always
    (b) Mostly
    (c) Half the time
    (d) Seems disinterested in children and/or resistant to feedback

4. HELPFULNESS:

    (a) Anticipates what needs to be done and does it
    (b) Responds when asked
    (c) Responds reluctantly
    (d) Does not help when asked

5. **PROFESSIONAL ETHICS AND DEMEANOR:**
   Maintains high ethical standards regarding children, families, and staff.
   Dresses and behaves appropriately.

   (a) Excellent
   (b) Good
   (c) Satisfactory
   (d) Unacceptable

6. **APPROPRIATE INTERACTION:**
   Uses positive guidance techniques to support play such as turn-taking and interactive match.

   (a) Always
   (b) Mostly
   (c) Needs improvement
   (d) Seems disengaged or uses directive language

7. **LAB/ENVIRONMENT KNOWLEDGE:**
   Awareness of lab procedures, was in assigned zone and performed assigned duties, asked questions for clarification of procedure when necessary, was concerned with children's health and safety.

   (a) Excellent
   (b) Good
   (c) Satisfactory
   (d) Needs improvement

8. **THE QUALITY WITHOUT A NAME:**
   Maintains enthusiasm for teaching on a daily basis. Makes an effort to establish relationships with the children. Exhibits insight.

   (a) Has fully developed this quality
   (b) Has developed this quality
   (c) Has somewhat developed this quality
   (d) Does not exhibit this quality

Teacher Comments:

INDEX

A

active learning, 1, 19, 62, 82, 92
activities have applications to different settings on/off campus, 64–5, 78–9, 81, 113, 130, 154, 171–2, 182, 186
application to other settings, 10, 14
application to the real world, 31
assessment, 11, 20, 27, 30, 63, 69–70, 83, 94, 99, 102–5, 114, 117, 118, 121, 124, 126, 128, 130, 134–6, 138, 139, 145, 667
assist with program evaluation, 32
authentic connections are made with peers, faculty, community, and/or the university, 33–4, 53, 65–6, 82, 130–1, 136, 140, 154, 186, 187

B

Bloom's taxonomy of learning, 154
building relationships through authentic connection, 41–2

C

case management activities, 21
case studies, 4, 21, 32
case study analysis, 20
CATME Peer Evaluation, 179
CATME Smarter Teamwork, 177
challenges, 20, 22, 23, 25–6, 32, 35, 40, 41, 46, 47, 86, 112, 113, 122–4, 128, 144, 146, 161, 169
child development, 22, 54, 74, 76–7, 91–108, 157, 169, 170
collaboration, 5, 24, 41, 47, 62, 66, 113, 116
communication, 13, 14, 31, 41, 47–9, 62, 97, 107, 112, 122, 128, 138, 167, 176, 177, 190, 192
community-based learning experiences, 52, 186
community organization(s), 62, 66, 67, 113, 121, 122, 124, 129, 130, 196
community partners, 46, 52, 53, 61, 66–7, 111–19, 122–6, 128, 130, 133–6, 139, 140, 176, 177, 186–92, 194, 196

community service, 46, 53–5, 58, 117, 154, 166, 172, 179, 185, 186, 190
considerable time spent on meaningful tasks, 24–5, 137
course design, 19–26, 63, 113, 135–6, 153–5, 157, 163
course instruction, 24
create a program, 32
Critical Reading and Integration Tests (CRITs), 125, 127, 128, 130
critical reflection, 167

D
designing curriculum, 24
Developmentally Appropriate Practice (DAP), 94, 95, 98, 100, 107
discussion(s), 12, 14, 21, 26, 29, 30, 34, 48, 69, 75, 92–7, 101, 112, 119, 123, 125, 127, 128, 135, 137–40, 144, 147, 154, 162, 167, 169, 170, 188–90, 194–6

E
evaluation, 32, 45, 48, 58, 69, 82, 84, 104, 105, 117–19, 121–31, 156, 158, 169, 170, 179, 180, 188
experiential activities, 19, 93, 195
experiential learning, 3, 10–11, 14, 16, 39, 40, 93, 122, 153, 165, 195

F
facilitate a learning group, 32
faculty and student peers interact about substantive matters, 30–1, 53, 64, 78, 81, 118–19, 154, 169–70, 186

family life education, 3–5, 9–16, 19–21, 30–2, 34, 40, 51, 52, 56, 73, 81–7, 91, 107, 111–19, 123, 133–40, 165–72, 190, 193, 195, 196, 199–206
family studies, 3, 5, 19–23, 25, 29, 33, 36, 40, 42, 43, 51–9, 82–7, 92, 124, 140, 148, 176
feedback through observation, 31
field-based experiences, 63, 144, 165, 166, 179, 196
field experience, 19–21, 34, 35, 54, 62, 64, 92, 103, 108, 166, 171, 195
field work, 19–23, 25, 26, 29, 195
Fink's taxonomy of significant learning, 154, 155
frequent performance feedback, 10, 14, 16, 21–2, 30, 78, 81, 87, 104–6, 117, 130, 136–40, 147–8, 154, 162, 181, 186, 188, 195, 196

G
Goldsmith's resource management model, 154–7
grant development model, 32
grant writing process, 186, 191, 196
group facilitation, 32

H
high-impact practices, 2–5, 9, 19, 20, 22, 25–6, 30–6, 51, 53, 62, 63, 81–7, 91, 92, 107, 111, 112, 116, 122, 136–40, 154, 158, 163, 180, 193–6
human systems theories, 11

I
immersion experience, 23
implementation, 2–4, 19, 20, 32, 40–2, 45–8, 66–70, 103, 111–13, 115, 125, 186, 191

interest, 4, 10, 11, 20, 34, 39, 55, 63, 64, 83, 86, 96, 100, 103, 113, 115, 123, 135, 155, 157, 158, 168, 177, 178, 182
internship, 2, 5, 9, 29–36, 39–49, 51–9, 61, 85, 116, 128, 145, 153, 166, 191, 194
   capstone internship, 20, 177
interview(s), 10, 13, 15–16, 20, 30, 31, 33, 45, 56, 57, 59, 61, 62, 65, 66, 68, 69, 83, 99, 100, 107, 117, 135, 195

J

journal(s)
   journal entries, 15, 21, 25, 26, 35, 44, 47, 138
   reflective writing, 31, 179

L

learning contract, 12, 14

M

meta-cognition, 21
methodology, 5, 81–7, 126, 133–40, 182, 195
Mezirow's theory of adult learning, 134
motivation, 6, 111, 177, 180, 196

N

networking opportunities, 10, 170
networking skills, 34

O

observations, 10, 11, 31, 47, 74–7, 79, 84, 91–7, 99–101, 103, 108, 125, 195
on-line journal, 14
out-of-class opportunities, 20, 166

P

personal growth, 23, 48, 172, 175
personal reflection, 25, 31
perspective transformation, 133–40
physical, cognitive, social and emotional development, 11, 97, 101
practicum, 2, 9–16, 93, 107, 166, 194, 195
pre-and-post assessments, 30
pre-internship, 10, 40, 53, 54, 62, 63, 65, 68, 69, 195
problem solving, 20, 41, 123, 167
professional awareness of attitudes, practices, and expectations, 10
professional behaviors, 10, 14
professional development, 21, 25, 39–49, 62–5, 68–70
professional training, 24, 52
program development, 30–2, 40, 121, 124, 125, 127, 128, 130
programming, 3–5, 15, 20, 32, 123, 133–40, 165–72, 189, 196
program outcomes, 5, 10, 28

R

real-world practice, 20, 31, 52, 53, 73, 106, 122, 170, 196
recommendations, 63, 122, 126, 148, 186, 191–2
reflection, 14–15, 25, 31, 32, 34, 44–7, 63, 69, 92, 94, 101, 121, 134, 137, 146, 154, 167, 169, 179, 182, 186, 189–90, 195
   guided reflection, 189
   reflection and feedback, 44–5, 195
   reflective journaling, 14
   reflective listening, 31
Reverse Planning Principles, 143–4

S

self-reflection, 10, 20, 22, 23, 25, 119, 122, 134

self-analysis, 20, 25, 105
seminars, 2, 21, 36, 54–6, 63, 69
   discussion seminars, 34
service-learning, 2, 5, 40, 45–9, 52, 53, 56, 81, 111, 117, 121, 133–40, 143–9, 153–63, 165–72, 175–82, 186, 194–6
simulation, 21, 23
structured journaling, 19, 195
student-constructed learning objectives, 34
student engagement, 25, 29, 33, 62, 63, 67, 93, 107
student interest and engagement, 11, 20, 25, 29, 33, 62, 63, 67, 93, 107, 157, 177
student lead, 30
student learning outcomes, 10
student-partner matching, 115
students experience diversity through contact with people different from themselves, 22–3, 34–6, 170–1
students receive frequent performance feedback, 78, 81, 104–6, 130, 147–8, 154, 181, 186, 188
students spend considerable amounts of time on meaningful tasks, 64, 77, 81, 127–8, 146–7, 154
support strategy, 26

T
teaching strategies, 25, 32
team and individual activities, 126–7
team building activities, 32
team presentations, 126, 127
team structure and development, 115–16
teamwork, 119, 124, 127, 177
technology, 65, 127
three course sequence, 29, 30, 36, 194
transaction, 167, 169, 196
transformation, 133–40, 167, 169, 172, 196
transmission, 167, 169, 196

V
video record and compare, 30
volunteer, 11, 21, 25, 42, 46, 56, 65, 67, 86, 112, 116, 117, 147, 153, 165, 171

W
writing assignment, 13, 15, 16, 191

Y
young children, 9, 46, 48, 86, 91–108

The manufacturer's authorised representative in the EU is Springer Nature Customer Service Centre GmbH, Europaplatz 3, 69115 Heidelberg, Germany. If you have any concerns regarding our products, please contact ProductSafety@springernature.com

Printed and bound by CPI Group (UK) Ltd, Croydon, CR0 4YY

23/03/2026

02076672-0004